— **Crust, mantle and core** →

Nature of boundaries

Compositions of regions

Physical properties of regions

Conrad discontinuity beneath continents due to granodiorite → granulite change.

} Compositional

CONTINENTAL: granodiorite overlying intermediate to basic granulite.
OCEANIC: basalt.

} basalt.

ined seismically he region above Mohorovičić ontinuity (Moho).

PHASE CHANGE TO HIGH-PRESSURE POLYMORPHS

Development of high-pressure phases, but still with composition of garnet.

ELOCITY ZONE: few % nelt; more prominent ceans.

Compositio resulting in solid → liqu

.JD (apart from -velocity zone): tic to passage of mic waves, but 1-state creep nits inelastic rmation beneath sphere and ·ection beneath osphere.

2885

Unless Recalled Earlier

Date Due

JUN 5 1987		
NOV 26 1991		
DEC -9 1992		

METAMORPHIC GEOLOGY

METAMORPHIC GEOLOGY

An introduction to tectonic and metamorphic processes

Con Gillen

University of Aberdeen

London
GEORGE ALLEN & UNWIN
Boston   Sydney

George Allen & Unwin (Publishers) Ltd,
40 Museum Street, London WC1A 1LU, UK

George Allen & Unwin (Publishers) Ltd,
Park Lane, Hemel Hempstead, Herts HP2 4TE, UK

Allen & Unwin Inc.,
9 Winchester Terrace, Winchester, Mass 01890, USA

George Allen & Unwin Australia Pty Ltd,
8 Napier Street, North Sydney, NSW 2060, Australia

First published in 1982

British Library Cataloguing in Publication Data

Gillen, Cornelius
  Metamorphic geology: an introduction to
  tectonic and metamorphic processes.
  1. Metamorphism (Geology)
  I. Title
  552   QE475.A2

  ISBN 0-04-551057-1
  ISBN 0-04-551058-X Pbk

QE
475
.A2
G53
1982

Library of Congress Cataloging in Publication Data

Gillen, Cornelius
  Metamorphic geology.

  Includes bibliographical references and index.
  1. Metamorphism (Geology) I. Title.
QE475.A2G53   552'.4   81-20514
ISBN 0-04-551057-1   AACR2
ISBN 0-04-551058-X (pbk.)

 # 845112O

Set in 10 on 12 Times by Preface Ltd, Salisbury, Wilts.
and printed in Great Britain by
Billing and Sons Ltd, Guildford, London and Worcester

Preface

This book is about metamorphic rocks: the processes involved in their formation and the reasons why they occur at particular places on the continents. It has been written to serve as an elementary text on the subjects of metamorphism and mountain building for non-specialist students of geology. It will be equally useful where geology is either the main or subsidiary subject and could be used by students intending to advance further in geology (the list of advanced texts in the further reading section would be more appropriate to such students). My intention in writing this book has been to try to dispel the notion that metamorphism comprises the 'haunted wing' of geology. Admittedly, there are rather a large number of technical terms in the book, but I hope that after working through it you will not find metamorphism an unduly difficult or obscure aspect of geology. Throughout, I have emphasised the strong links between mountain building, plate tectonics and metamorphic processes.

The book introduces metamorphic rocks by considering their textures and field relations, then moves on to deal with the factors controlling metamorphism. Case studies of areas of metamorphic rocks are then presented in the context of modern theories of the Earth's activity, and the place of metamorphic rocks in the formation of ancient and young mountain belts is analysed.

New technical terms and concepts are explained in context as they are introduced, important terms being emphasised in **bold** print. Most of the terms in bold are again defined in the Glossary, which, together with the Index, should be used freely as you progress through the book to look back at definitions and explanations. Each chapter concludes with a brief summary and a few exercises, which should be attempted before consulting the answers (which are only a guide and not necessarily definitive or the only 'correct' ones).

Frequent references are made to hand specimens of rocks and it is recommended that a rock collection should contain the following as a minimum: slate or phyllite, schist, banded gneiss, hornfels, quartzite and marble. Itineraries for field excursions are not given, since the list of guides in the Further Reading section should provide sufficient ideas. Care should be taken in the field to follow the best rules of conduct; indiscriminate hammering of localities should be discouraged, and collections made in the field should be properly labelled in the laboratory or classroom.

C. GILLEN   August 1981

Acknowledgements

I wish to thank most sincerely Roger Jones of George Allen & Unwin for his assistance and patience during the long gestation of this work. The series editors, Dr and Mrs Wilson and the reviewers, Mr N. Bates, Dr S. Drury, Professor J. Watson and Mr P. Whitehead have made numerous valuable suggestions and helpful criticisms, for which I am most grateful.

I should also like to record my thanks to Mr P. O'Donoghue, University College Dublin, for helping with photographs.

Grateful acknowledgement is made to those who have given permission to use figures from the following sources:

Inside covers: Brown, G. C. and A. E. Mussett 1981. *The inaccessible Earth*. London: George Allen & Unwin.

Fig. 1.1: Open University Course Team 1970. *S100, Science: a foundation course*. Milton Keynes: The Open University.

Fig. 2.6: Wyllie, J. 1976. *The way the Earth works*. New York: Wiley.

Fig. 3.3: Eastwood, T. 1968. *Geology of the country around Cockermouth and Calbeck*. London: Institute of Geological Sciences.

Figs 3.9, 3.10, 3.12: Sibson, R. H. 1977. Fault rocks and fault mechanisms. *J. Geol. Soc. Lond.* **133**.

Fig. 3.13: George, T. N. 1965. The geological growth of Scotland. In *The geology of Scotland*, G. Y. Craig (ed.). Edinburgh: Oliver & Boyd.

Fig. 3.14: McClay, K. R. and M. P. Coward 1981. The Moine Thrust Zone. An overview. In *Thrust and nappe tectonics*. Geol. Soc. Sp. Publ. no. 9. London: Geological Society.

Figs 4.1, 4.6: Read, H. H. and J. Watson 1975. Part 1: Early stages of Earth history. In *Introduction to geology*, Vol. 2: *Earth history*. London: Macmillan.

Fig. 4.5: Winchester, J. A. 1974. The regional metamorphic zones in the Scottish Caledonides. *J. Geol. Soc. Lond.* **130**, 509–24.

Fig. 4.8: Roberts, J. L. and J. E. Treagus 1977. The Dalradian rocks of the South-west Highlands – Introduction. *Scott. J. Geol.* **13**, 87–100.

Figs 4.14, 4.17: Miyashiro, A. 1973. *Metamorphism and metamorphic belts*. London: George Allen & Unwin.

Figs 5.3, 5.4: Anderton, R. *et al.* 1979. *A dynamic stratigraphy of the British Isles*. London: George Allen & Unwin.

Fig. 6.3: Johnson, M. R. W. 1963. *Geol. en mijnbouw*. **5**, 121–42.

Contents

List of tables

1 Introduction

What are metamorphic rocks?

The word metamorphism stems from Greek roots and literally means 'change of form'. Metamorphic rocks have been produced by physical and chemical changes that have affected other rocks. By now you will have met the other two fundamental divisions into igneous and sedimentary rocks. Each of the three major classes was produced by quite different processes in the Earth and as a result each has certain characteristic features. Igneous rocks were formed by the crystallisation of silicate melts. Since crystals in a melt can grow equally in all directions, the silicate minerals of such rocks interlock with each other in all directions. In the case of sedimentary rocks, particles or fragments are usually cemented together. The fragments were transported over the surface of the Earth and eventually deposited as loose sediment, and later packing and cementing of the grains produced solid rock. Sedimentary rocks are often arranged in parallel, sheet-like layers or beds and they may contain fossils. Metamorphic rocks are produced when other – pre-existing – rocks are affected, mainly by increases in pressure and temperature, which can happen only at considerable depths in the Earth's crust. Metamorphic rocks were never molten at any stage in their development. Instead, they formed in the solid state under conditions of high stress, as a result of which their crystals may sometimes have grown in parallel alignment.

At this point you may well be wondering what is the source of the heat and pressure that cause rocks to be metamorphosed. It is known from direct observation that pressure and temperature increase with depth in the Earth. The rate at which temperature changes with depth is known as the **geothermal gradient**. The geothermal gradient itself varies with depth, the gradient being a tangent to the **geotherm** or the depth v. temperature curve for the Earth. In any study of the causes of metamorphism the geotherm and the geothermal gradient are basic factors that must be taken into account. Since temperature increases with depth, there has to be a heat source. In the crust, this heat source is provided by the decay or breakdown of **radioactive isotopes** present in rocks, with the release of heat energy. Heat or thermal energy is one factor which causes chemical reactions to take place within and between minerals, resulting in the formation of new minerals.

Metamorphic rocks are thought to account for a huge proportion of the continental crust, although over vast areas such as the Russian Platform the metamorphic rocks forming the **basement** are buried by younger, often sedimentary, formations. The cores of all the continents – the shield areas older than 600 Ma (millions of years) – are built almost exclusively of metamorphic rocks, and most of the world's oldest rocks are metamorphic. **Fold mountain** chains such as the Alps and the Himalayas contain large amounts of metamorphic rocks, which were deformed by folding, faulting and thrusting and were intruded by large volumes of granite magma. The fact that metamorphic rocks are nearly always deformed indicates that there is a strong relationship between metamorphism and **tectonic** (or mountain building) processes.

From your experience in the field you are no doubt aware that rocks at the surface tend to be weathered. Many of the silicates in igneous rocks are broken down physically, chemically and biologically and are replaced by other minerals, which are stable at the Earth's surface, depending on the climate. In sedimentary rocks the cement may have been dissolved away, allowing the grains in the rock to fall out rather easily. These changes take place at normal temperatures on the Earth's surface but they do not constitute metamorphism according to the definition used here. Changes take place also in loose sediments as they are transformed into sedimentary rocks during burial. The process of **diagenesis** involves compaction and cementation of the grains, coupled with various textural changes in the transition to a sedimentary rock. These are also near-surface processes that occur at normal pressure and temperatures in sedimentary basins (lakes, seas and oceans). Sediments are not heated up much as they become the kinds of sedimentary rocks you might see in South-east England, for example. Therefore, diagenesis is usually excluded from the definition of metamorphism. Notice though that very deeply buried sediments may be heated up to over 100 °C and their grains may be slightly flattened due to the load of overlying rocks. Metamorphism belongs to the Earth's internal processes and involves changes in the texture and mineralogy of the original grains in the rocks of the crust. Apart from water, practically nothing enters or leaves a rock mass (or **system**) during metamorphism. No overall chemical changes occur; the original constituents are just rearranged differently during **recrystallisation**.

The important factors that control metamorphism are pressure due to depth in the crust, temperature, **strain** (shape and volume changes due to **stress** during deformation) and **fluid activity** (or the pressure due to fluids such as water and carbon dioxide in pore spaces). All these factors can vary from place to place in the crust and they result in quite different types of metamorphism, depending on the dominant factors in a particular situation. Using the variables temperature, pressure, strain and fluid pressure, metamorphism can be classified as follows:

(a) High temperature, low pressure, low strain and variable fluid pressure (also known as **thermal** or **contact** metamorphism);
(b) high strain, variable pressure, variable temperature and high fluid pressure (also known as **dynamic** metamorphism);
(c) high temperature, high pressure, variable strain and variable fluid pressure (also known as **regional** metamorphism).

These three types overlap considerably. Thermal and dynamic metamorphism may be thought of as special cases, restricted to localised areas. As the name suggests, regional metamorphism affects rocks over wide areas of the crust – several tens of thousands of square kilometres – whereas contact and dynamic metamorphism are more local in their effects. Contact metamorphism is restricted to zones a few hundred metres wide around large igneous intrusions, where temperatures are greatly increased for a brief time. Dynamic metamorphic effects occur

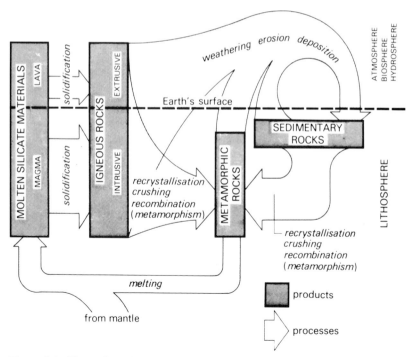

Figure 1.1 The rock cycle.

only along fault and thrust zones, a few tens of metres thick, in which rocks are highly strained because of fault movement; fault planes act as channelways for fluids, particularly water, so that high fluid activity is a characteristic feature. The minerals, **structures** and **textures** (how grains relate to each other) in rocks formed under these different metamorphic conditions are quite distinct.

The boundary between diagenesis and metamorphism on the one hand and between metamorphism and magma formation by rock melting on the other, is not particularly sharp and distinct. Rather, there are gradations which may be summarised as follows:

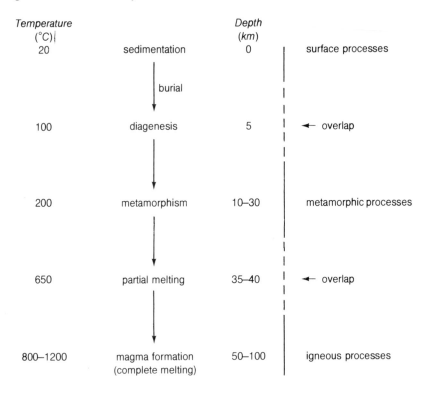

The figures in the above scheme are approximate and are quoted merely to give an impression of the order of magnitude. Actual values vary widely in different parts of the crust and are affected by rock composition, stress, fluid activity and heat flow.

The overlap between metamorphic and surface and igneous processes indicates that metamorphism plays a central role in the study of dynamic processes in the Earth's crust. Modern plate tectonic views on the Earth's mobility help to explain the occurrence of metamorphic rocks on the continental side of ocean/continent destructive margins and in continental collison zones. Various igneous rocks are found in these situations, and there is a close interrelation between igneous, metamorphic and tectonic processes in the crust, as may be seen from considering the **rock cycle** (Fig. 1.1).

What does a metamorphic rock look like?

Metamorphic rocks are distinctive in the field and in the laboratory. They are **crystalline** rocks, which makes them generally strong and hard. Most of the minerals in metamorphic rocks are silicates, a few of which are restricted to metamorphic rocks, but others are common to igneous and some sedimentary rocks. The texture of a metamorphic rock is its most distinguishing feature. The commonest examples have a well defined parallel arrangement of minerals, which allows the rock to be split into sheets or plates. Metamorphic rocks often have a banded or striped appearance, with different minerals in the various bands. One notable feature of metamorphic processes is that they tend to produce a fairly limited number of rock types. Areas of metamorphic rocks of different ages around the world often contain quite similar rocks.

The make-up of metamorphic rocks

There are two essential features of any rock that must be described: mineral content and texture. Grain size and structure are also important. Since metamorphic rocks are derived from other rocks, it is natural to expect minerals that are common to different rock types. In addition, there are a number of silicate minerals which are restricted to metamorphic rocks.

The situation may be summarised as follows:

Minerals common to metamorphic and igneous rocks	quartz, feldspar, muscovite, biotite, hornblende, pyroxene, olivine, iron ore
Minerals common to metamorphic and sedimentary rocks	quartz, muscovite, clay minerals, calcite, dolomite

Minerals found in   garnet, andalusite, kyanite, sillimanite,
metamorphic rocks   staurolite, cordierite, epidote, chlorite
only (or mainly)

Minerals specific to metamorphic rocks are described in the Glossary and are illustrated in Table 1.1. You will have come across the other minerals before, and they will not be described in any great detail here.

Metamorphic rock textures

The most striking aspect of a metamorphic rock is its texture – the relationship between individual grains. Metamorphic rocks are crystalline, with crystals either interlocking in a **random** fashion to produce a massive rock or arranged in an ordered fashion. At first sight it is possible for a massive metamorphic rock to resemble another rock type, such as a dolomite or a limestone. On the other hand, metamorphic rocks often possess **directional fabrics**, in which minerals are arranged in parallel alignment. Micas and other platy minerals may define a **planar fabric**, whereas minerals growing as long blades or rods may define a **linear fabric**. A metamorphic rock containing hornblende and biotite, for example, might have both planar and linear fabrics. These **preferred orientations**, which arise because of deformation and recrystallisation during metamorphism, have special names. Planar fabrics are referred to as **foliations**, and linear fabrics are called **lineations** (Fig. 1.2).

Metamorphic rocks may be described according to grain size, just as for igneous and sedimentary rocks, with the following subdivisions:

(a) fine-grained: grains less than 0.1 mm in diameter;
(b) medium-grained: grains between 0.1 and 1.0 mm in diameter;
(c) coarse-grained: grains over 1.0 mm in diameter.

These grain-size terms refer to rocks with or without directional fabrics. In the case of foliated rocks, a further set of names is used to describe the various planar fabrics. Commonly used foliation fabric terms are:

(a) **cleavage (slaty cleavage)** in fine-grained rocks;
(b) **schistosity** in medium-grained rocks;
(c) **bonding (gneissore bonding)** in coarse-grained rocks.

It is the arrangement of mineral grains or groups of grains that gives rise to a fabric in a metamorphic rock. For example, a schistosity may be

Table 1.1 Physical properties of metamorphic minerals.

Name	Composition	System	Form	Habit	Colour	Other properties
andalusite	Al_2SiO_5	orthorhombic	basal sections of chiastolite	prismatic	pale brown	usually covered by layers of mica
kyanite	Al_2SiO_5	triclinic		bladed (prismatic)	pale blue	
sillimanite	Al_2SiO_5	orthorhombic		prismatic (acicular)	pale straw	
garnet	$X_3Al_2Si_3O_{12}$ X = Mg, Fe, Ca, Mn	cubic	icositetrahedron, dodecahedron	euhedral crystals	red, black, green, etc.	isotropic, may contain inclusions
staurolite	$(FeMg)_2(AlFe)_9Si_4O_{22}(OH)_2$	monoclinic (pseudo-orthorhombic)		squat prismatic	dark brown	
cordierite	$(MgFe)_2Al_4Si_5O_{18}$	orthorhombic (pseudo-hexagonal)	cyclic twinning produces a crystal with a hexagonal appearance	prismatic	deep blue	inclusions of zircon give pleochroic haloes (thin sect.)

Figure 1.2   Pronounced lineation on the foliation surface of a gneiss. Lewisian Gneiss Complex.

defined by platy quartz or a lineation by rod-shaped quartz–feldspar intergrowths. A directional fabric is a metamorphic texture in which crystals of the metamorphic **mineral assemblage** display preferred orientation due to deformation and recrystallisation. That is, crystals 'prefer' to grow parallel to the direction of minimum stress because less energy is required to grow that way.

Two further textural terms are used to describe metamorphic rocks. If the rock is even-grained, i.e. all the crystals are approximately the same size and equidimensional, it is said to have a **granoblastic** texture. A metamorphic rock with a granoblastic texture does not possess a foliation as well, because, if the grains are equidimensional, there can be no preferred orientation. Garnet, quartz, feldspar, pyroxene and olivine are common examples of silicates with nearly equidimensional crystal shapes. Compare these with hornblende (acicular or needle-shaped) or with biotite and muscovite (sheet-like). Some rocks may have large crystals (or *porphyroblasts*) set in a finer-grained matrix; such rocks are described as having a **porphyroblastic** texture. Compare these terms with the phenocrysts in a porphyritic igneous rock. Rocks with a porphyroblastic texture may also be foliated, a good example being garnet–mica schist, in which the garnet porphyroblasts are larger than the mica flakes which are in parallel alignment (Fig. 1.3). A special variety

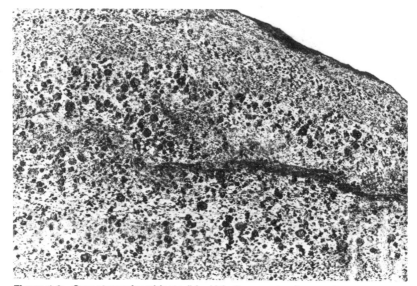

Figure 1.3   Garnet porphyroblasts (black) in finer-grained groundmass.

of porphyroblastic texture may be found in some very coarse-grained granitic gneisses in which large porphyroblasts of feldspar are surrounded by smaller feldspar, quartz and mica crystals, giving the overall appearance of an eye. Such rocks are usually coarsely banded and are called **augen gneisses** (*auge* is the German word for 'eye'). Augen gneisses may also develop from the deformation of granites, in which case the feldspar augen were originally phenocrysts, which were partly granulated (or fragmented) during strong deformation. In such cases the augen are referred to as *porphyroclasts* (Fig. 1.4).

Metamorphism tends to obliterate original structures in rocks, such as cross-bedding in sediments, with the result that metamorphic rocks can appear quite similar although they may be of different ages and from different parts of the world.

Many metamorphic rocks have a fairly simple mineral composition. The term 'mineral assemblage' is used to describe all the minerals in a rock. In metamorphic rocks it is assumed that the minerals are in **equilibrium** with each other. Equilibrium or **stable** assemblages are achieved when a particular temperature and pressure are maintained for a sufficient length of time to allow all the minerals of an assemblage to crystallise and reach stability with one another. Mineral assemblages of metamorphic rocks consist of rather few dominant minerals, up to four

Figure 1.4   Hand specimen of augen gneiss. Large pale coloured porphyroclasts of feldspar; biotite is black; weakly foliated but not banded.

or five being usual. Here are a few examples:

Rock name	Possible mineral assemblage
quartzite	quartz
schist	mica + quartz + garnet
marble	calcite + olivine + pyroxene
gneiss	feldspar + quartz + amphibole + mica

The list of minerals in an assemblage is written in decreasing order of abundance. It should be possible to recognise most or all of the minerals in a metamorphic rock in the field or in a laboratory hand specimen.

The major minerals of metamorphic rocks are silicates of aluminium (Al), iron (Fe), magnesium (Mg), calcium (Ca), sodium (Na) and potassium (K). Non-silicates are calcium and magnesium carbonates and iron oxides (iron ores). In addition, water, carbon dioxide and a few other fluids are important in metamorphic processes; these fluids are important during the progress of metamorphic reactions, but they may not appear in the final rock products.

Metamorphic reactions

If pressure and temperature conditions steadily increase during metamorphism, the resulting metamorphic mineral assemblages of the rocks form part of a **progressive metamorphic sequence**. The metamorphism is usually described as **prograde**. If subsequently the same rocks are subjected to a second episode of metamorphism at a lower temperature than the first and (often) with the introduction of water, the metamorphism is termed **retrograde**. During retrograde metamorphism an earlier mineral assemblage is replaced or partially replaced by a new assemblage that is stable under the new conditions.

The changes that occur during metamorphism are the results of chemical **reactions** between some or all of the rock components. Metamorphic reactions are of two main types, i.e.:

(a) solid → solid + vapour;
(b) solid → solid;

where the arrow indicates the direction of the reaction. Individual components are referred to as **phases**, where solid phases are crystals and **vapour** phases are fluids such as water (H_2O) or carbon dioxide (CO_2). Vapour phases are **mobile**, i.e. they can move between and around solid phases and they can enter or leave the entire system. Reactions of type (a) which involve the loss of water (water appears on the right hand side of the equation and is a product of the reaction) are called **dehydration** reactions, or **decarbonation** reactions if carbon dioxide is the vapour phase. Dehydration reactions are common in the prograde (or progressive) metamorphism of rocks that initially contain water, e.g. shales. Decarbonation occurs during the metamorphism of carbonate rocks such as limestone. Retrogressive (or retrograde) metamorphism often involves the addition of water, the reaction being referred to as **hydration**, i.e.:

$$\text{solid} + H_2O \rightarrow \text{(hydrated) solid}$$

Some metamorphic reactions (type (b)) involve only solid phases, an important example being the **transformation** of kyanite (Al_2SiO_5) to sillimanite (also Al_2SiO_5). This reaction depends on an increase in temperature and does not involve a change in composition, only crystal structure (kyanite has triclinic symmetry, sillimanite has orthorhombic symmetry). Minerals with the same composition but different crystal structures are termed **polymorphs**. Andalusite, kyanite and sillimanite are polymorphs of Al_2SiO_5 (aluminium silicate). Not all solid–solid reactions involve polymorphs, of course, as new minerals are generally formed during metamorphism. The study of metamorphic reactions is an important branch of the subject in that it provides vital information about the pressure and temperature conditions of metamorphism.

Field relations of metamorphic rocks

Each of the main types of metamorphism gives rise to cetain varieties of rock which may be restricted to particular geological environments. Contact metamorphic rocks are found in the heat-affected zones or **aureoles** around large igneous intrusions, and rocks that have suffered dynamic metamorphism are restricted to fault and thrust zones. Regional metamorphic rocks occupy large areas of mountain chains and they form the basement rocks of the continents.

When an area is being investigated in the field, the geologist has to establish the broad **field relations** – how the various rock types and structures relate to each other in space. The presence of a plutonic intrusion or of a major thrust might lead him to expect to find contact and dynamic metamorphic rocks, of local extent, in the area. Folded and highly deformed rocks beneath, for example, an angular unconformity could possibly have been metamorphosed at high pressure and temperature. Care must be taken, though, to avoid preconceived ideas about particular rock types in such environments, as this might lead to misidentification in the field. For example, not all folded rocks are metamorphic; small igneous intrusions may cause only baking of adjacent sediments; and faults with small displacements will not have produced mylonites (recrystallised milled rock).

Hard, brittle rocks called **hornfelses** are found in contact metamorphic aureoles. They have a crystalline texture and they break into sharp, angular, glassy-looking fragments. Hornfelses are harder than the unaffected surrounding **country rocks** and they may form features on the landscape around an intrusion, and veins and dykes from plutons may penetrate the country rocks.

Dynamic metamorphic rocks are produced by fracturing, grinding and streaking out of pre-existing rocks. Typical products are **breccia**, with angular fragments, and **mylonite**, a hard, fine-grained flinty rock which may be banded and which contains porphyroclasts of the country rock in a recrystallised cement.

Regional metamorphic rocks are the commonest kind of metamorphic rock. They are widespread on the continents and they span the entire geological column, though since they are formed at depth they are seen only in deeply eroded areas. In the field, regional metamorphic rocks are recognised by having oriented fabrics, both planar and linear. They are often coarsely crystalline, even-grained or porphyroblastic and intricately folded. There is frequently an association between pegmatites, granite intrusions and regionally metamorphosed rocks such as gneisses.

When describing a metamorphic rock in the field, it is essential to identify and note the following features:

(a) original features such as bedding or lava flows;
(b) minerals present in order of abundance;
(c) rock texture, grain size and fabric;
(d) structures such as folds and faults;
(e) igneous features such as intrusions in the vicinity.

The flow chart in Table 1.2 is designed to help you identify ten common metamorphic rocks. Since the chart cannot cover all possible rock varieties, the definitions and descriptions in the Glossary should be used as a check against your identifications.

Uses of metamorphic rocks

Two common metamorphic rocks that are likely to be found in any town are **slate** on roofs and **marble** as an ornamental facing stone on buildings. The large number of disused slate quarries in Wales and Scotland indicate that it is no longer economical to work slate as a roofing material, although crushed slate has recently been put to use in the building industry. Some minerals occurring in metamorphic rocks are used in insulating buildings. The most well known of these is **asbestos**, a fibrous mineral which originates from the alteration of certain amphiboles. It can be powdered, woven or pressed into sheets and it is extremely versatile. Unfortunately, when in the form of very fine powder, individual particles of the mineral can be inhaled and they settle on the lining of the lung. This can cause irritation and eventual disease. **Talc** is a widely used lubricating material of metamorphic origin. Talc is a very soft, platy mineral (hardness 1 on Mohs' scale), which occurs in talc schists (metamorphosed ultrabasic igneous rocks).

A few minerals in metamorphic rocks can be cut, faceted, polished and mounted as semi-precious stones. Diamond is a precious stone which forms under very high pressure. It is occasionally found in metamorphic rocks but its most usual occurrence is in kimberlite, which is a volcanic rock. Certain garnets are used as gems if they are perfect and flawless with good colour and lustre. Marble, particularly the pale green variety, is often cut, polished and mounted to make pendants and rings. Tiger's eye is a variety of crocidolite, which is related to asbestos (Fig. 1.5). Crocidolite is silicified but still retains the asbestos-type fibres (although they cannot be teased apart). When polished, crocidolite takes on an exceptionally lustrous sheen.

Table 1.2 Flow chart for identifying common metamorphic rocks.

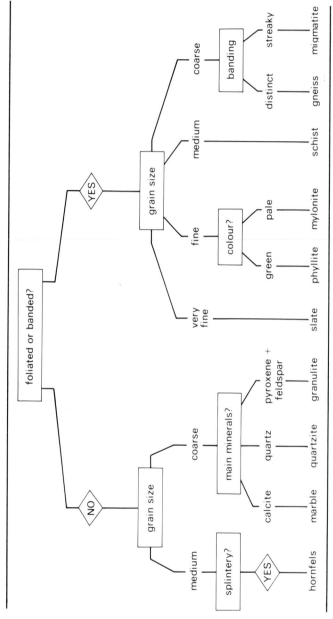

Figure 1.5   (a) Asbestos, showing fibres; (b) crocidolite (Tiger's eye) or silicified asbestos.

What this book is about

The main aims of this book are to help you to understand the principles of metamorphism – how, why and where rocks are metamorphosed in the crust – and to outline the metamorphic structure of orogenic belts. You will learn something about the way temperature and heat flow vary with depth in the crust, both at the present time and in the geological past. A study of metamorphic rocks in shield areas and orogenic belts provides vital information that is relevant to theories concerning the early evolution of the crust. Also, metamorphic reactions tell us about the pressure and temperature conditions that prevailed during mountain building.

We lay the foundations for studying metamorphism by examining certain basic concepts concerning heat flow and sources of heat in the crust, stress, strain, crystal growth and chemical reactions. Do not be alarmed by these terms; the concepts are clearly explained and gradually developed in the text. After examining the factors that control metamorphism we move on to deal with the processes responsible for different types of metamorphism in a variety of geological environments: mountain belts, shields, thrust zones, igneous intrusions and subduction zones, which will be examined from the points of view of plate tectonics and the evolution of the Earth. Finally, the relative dating of metamorphic events and geothermal evolution will be examined, with metamorphic textures being related to structures in the field.

This book is neither a laboratory manual nor a field guide, but suggestions for field work and laboratory exercises on metamorphic rocks are given. Remember to use the Glossary and Index freely: these are integral parts of the book and should be used to locate an item in the text or check up on a definition. By the time you approach this text, you will have studied several other aspects of geology, so that many scientific concepts, mineral and rock names, etc. will already be quite familiar.

Summary

Metamorphic rocks are those which have been derived from the combined action of heat, pressure, strain and fluids on pre-existing rocks. They consist in the main of silicate minerals, which display random or oriented (directional) fabrics. Directional fabrics are planar (foliations) or linear (lineations). The set of co-existing minerals in a metamorphic rock is called the mineral assemblage.

During metamorphism, chemical reactions between components take place to produce a new mineral assemblage. Apart from water and carbon dioxide, very little material enters or leaves a rock mass during metamorphism. Progressive metamorphic sequences usually involve the gradual dehydration or decarbonation of a rock mass. Hydration is a characteristic feature of retrogressive metamorphism.

Different types of metamorphic rock are restricted to, or are characteristic of, certain geological environments in the crust. High-temperature–low-pressure (contact or thermal) metamorphism takes place in aureoles surrounding large igneous intrusions. High-pressure, high-strain, variable-temperature (dynamic) metamorphism is characteristic of thrust zones. High-pressure–high-temperature (regional) metamorphism takes place over very broad areas of the crust and is responsible for producing the rocks that make up much of continental shield areas and the deeper parts of mountain chains.

Exercise

Give complete descriptions of the following metamorphic rocks in hand specimen, and check your answers with the descriptions given in the Glossary: slate, mica schist, phyllite, gneiss, marble, quartzite, mylonite.

2 How rocks are changed

The factors controlling metamorphism

The Earth's heat

Since all metamorphic rocks require, or are associated with, the action of heat during their formation, it is necessary to investigate the source of this heat.

The temperature at the Earth's surface is 10–20 °C on average, although in polar regions and on high mountains it is much colder, while in deep mines it is too hot to work for long periods. Temperature obviously varies with depth. In addition, there are hot springs in areas of recent volcanic activity where water emerging from springs is heated up inside the crust. So the temperature in the Earth's crust increases with increasing depth. The temperature change (in °C) with depth (in km) can be plotted on a graph to give a curve, referred to as the geotherm. Plot such a graph, using the figures in the following table (Table 2.1). Use a scale of 1 cm ≡ 1 km vertically and 1 cm ≡ 50 °C horizontally; plot T °C from left to right, depth in km down the vertical axis (this may seem strange at first, but it is more convenient to plot depth in the crust downwards).

The graph is not a straight line, but a curve, the **geothermal curve** or geotherm (Fig. 2.1). The slope of this curve, i.e. the tangent to it, is called the geothermal gradient which is the rate at which temperature increases with depth in a particular region, i.e.:

$$\text{geothermal gradient} = \frac{\text{change in temperature}}{\text{change in depth}} \, °C \, km^{-1}$$

Notice that the rate of temperature increase is large at first, but decreases with depth.

Table 2.1 Variation in temperature with depth in crust.

Depth (km)	0	1	2	3	4	5	6	7	8	9	10
Temperature (T °C)	15	60	110	150	180	215	230	250	265	275	285

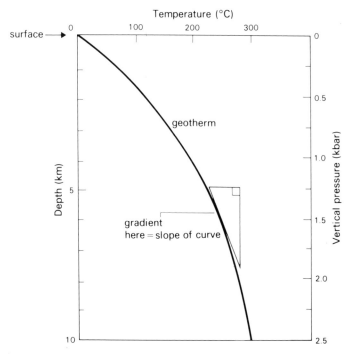

Figure 2.1 Temperature plotted against depth in the crust. The resulting curve is called the geotherm and the tangent to it gives the local geothermal gradient.

Where does the heat come from?

From the graph in Figure 2.1 it can be seen that temperature increases with depth in the Earth. The heat from the Sun is not sufficient to cause this, so a **heat source** is necessary. The main energy source in the Earth responsible for internal processes, including metamorphism and mountain building, is the heat energy released by the decay or breakdown of **radioactive elements**. Elements have **isotopes** (atoms of the same element but with different mass), some of which are radioactive (that is they are unstable and decay with time) producing heat and more stable isotopes. Some elements in rocks of the Earth's crust and mantle have long-lived isotopes, i.e. their **half lives** (time taken for half the atoms of a radioactive isotope to disintegrate) are very long and they break down slowly. Potassium-40 (^{40}K), uranium-238 (^{238}U) and thorium-232 (^{232}Th) are the most important isotopes for heat production in the Earth. The uranium isotope ^{235}U was most important for heat production in the

Table 2.2   Important radioactive isotopes.

Radioactive isotope	Half life (Ma)	Heat production (hpu)
uranium-238	4 500	2.30
thorium-232	13 900	0.63
potassium-40	1 300	0.67

early history of the Earth. Tables 2.2 and 2.3 show these isotopes with their breakdown products, half lives in millions of years (Ma) and abundances or amounts present in rocks in parts per million (ppm, equivalent to grams per tonne) in different rocks. Notice that all three isotopes are more abundant in acid rocks than in basic rocks, because they have become concentrated in acid rocks by various processes over a long period of time. Because these isotopes have been decaying since the origin of the Earth some 4600 Ma ago, they must have been more abundant then. Thorium, with the longest half life, would have been only a little more abundant, uranium about twice its present amount, and potassium-40 some ten times as abundant as it is today. Why was potassium-40 so very much more abundant? The answer is that it has the shortest half life of the three, and so must have decayed more rapidly. It also follows that much more heat was being produced in the early stages of the Earth's history by the decay of these isotopes.

How does the heat travel?

Within the solid outer part of the Earth (the **lithosphere**) heat travels mainly by **conduction**: heat energy is transmitted from particle to particle due to molecular vibrations induced by thermal energy. In addition, heat may be transferred relatively quickly by the upward movement of

Table 2.3   Average concentrations of radioactive isotopes in crustal and mantle rocks.

Rock type	Average concentration (ppm)			Total heat production (hpu)
	U-238	Th-232	K-40	
sediments	3.00	8.00	1 500	1.50
acid igneous rocks	4.75	18.50	38 000	2.50
basic igneous rocks	0.60	2.70	8 000	0.30
metamorphic granulite	0.40	2.10	22 000	0.30
typical mantle rocks	0.02	0.05	10	0.01

magma, or by circulating hot water and gases (**hydrothermal** fluids), as well as by the movements of blocks of the crust along faults. Beneath the lithosphere, in the upper mantle, heat is thought to travel mainly in **convection currents** in a very viscous (or thick and sticky) material. Much of the heat from the mantle thus enters the base of the crust, and, together with the heat being generated within the crust, is then transmitted upwards by conduction. The rate at which heat can be transmitted depends on the **conductivity** of rocks. This property is familiar enough in everyday life, if you consider the following. Touch a window pane, a piece of metal, a wooden table and a piece of cloth in the room where you are at the moment. Notice that the metal feels coldest, then the glass, the wood, and finally, the cloth seems warmest. Why is this, when all the items in the room are at the same temperature, and your hand has a constant temperature? The materials must remove some of the heat from your hand at different rates, depending on the conductivity of the material. Metal is a good conductor of heat, and feels cold to the touch; cloth is a good insulator (poor conductor) and so feels warm. Within the lithosphere, heat flows upwards by conduction towards the surface. Different rocks conduct heat at different rates, just as other materials do. **Heat flow** at the surface of the Earth is the total of all the heat produced within and below the crust.

Heat flow

Heat flow varies around the world, depending on the nature and age of the geological province where the heat flow is measured. Table 2.4

Table 2.4 Heat flow distribution in various crustal tectonic provinces.

Crustal province	Heat flow (hfu)	Average age (Ma)
Precambrian continental shield	0.90	2000
stable continental platform	1.00	1000
Caledonian orogenic belt	1.10	400
Hercynian orogenic belt	1.25	300
Mesozoic orogenic belt	1.40	200
Cenozoic orogenic belt	1.75	50
modern volcanic zone	2.20	0
ocean basin	1.30	50
oceanic ridge	2.00	0
oceanic trench	1.20	150

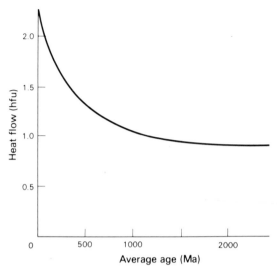

Figure 2.2   Heat flow plotted against age of continental crust.

shows the heat flow distribution in different continental and oceanic tectonic provinces, together with the ages of the provinces. Heat flow may be expressed in SI units of $W\,m^{-2}$ (watts per square metre), although it is more convenient to work in **heat flow units (hfu)**, where:

$$41.8\ \text{hfu} = 1.0\ W\,m^{-2}$$

Using the information for continents given in Table 2.4, plot heat flow vertically against age of province horizontally, in Ma (suggested scales: 2 cm ≡ 0.5 hfu, 4 cm ≡ 500 Ma). Join the points on the graph to give a smooth curve and note carefully its shape. We shall return to this curve again in a later section. Compare your graph with Figure 2.2. The main feature to be noticed is that the average heat flow through continental orogenic provinces decreases from 1.5 hfu for the Mesozoic to 1.0 hfu for Precambrian shields, i.e. modern heat flow is related to the age of rocks. A similar pattern emerges for oceanic heat flow.

The geothermal gradient

The geothermal gradient is the slope of the tangent to the geotherm (Fig. 2.1). The increase in temperature with depth is measured in degrees Celsius per kilometre (i.e. $T\ ^\circ C\ km^{-1}$) which is the unit of meas-

Table 2.5 Geothermal gradient in various crustal environments.

Type of crust	Geothermal gradient ($^{\circ}C\ km^{-1}$)
Gulf Coast, USA (oil wells)	30
Middle East (oil wells)	50
active volcanic zones (modern)	100
oceanic trenches (subduction zones)	10
Precambrian shields today	20–25
sialic crust in the Archaean	50

urement of the geothermal gradient. The temperature gradient varies from place to place in the crust, depending on the geological environment, and it has also varied at different times in the Earth's history. It is occasionally possible to measure the gradient directly, in mines and deep oil wells for example. Table 2.5 shows some values of the present geothermal gradient measured in regions of different ages. As might be expected, the gradient in volcanic zones is steep, but in ocean trenches it is shallow. The continental average is usually taken to be about 20–25 $^{\circ}$C km^{-1}. Refer back to Figure 2.1 and notice again the shape of the geotherm: the gradient decreases with depth. This is the case because heat-producing elements are **depleted** (or reduced in amount) in the deep crust, otherwise rocks would melt at very shallow depths owing to a rapid build-up of heat. Note that Table 2.5 gives values of the gradient at the Earth's surface. From the table, you will also note that the gradient in the early part of the Earth's history, during the Archaean (4600–2500 Ma ago), was steep. Heat flow in the early history of the Earth may have been higher than at present, owing to the greater effect of heat from the more abundant radioactive isotopes. However, in Chapter 4 it will be suggested that the ancient geothermal gradient may not have been much steeper than the present-day gradient, owing to the greater loss of heat from ancient **constructive plate margins**.

Pressure in the Earth

The second major controlling influence on metamorphic processes is **pressure**, but the term 'pressure' covers several different kinds of force acting in the Earth. Pressure is force per unit area acting on a surface.

Total pressure in the crust is made up of **confining pressure**, which is related to depth, and the pressure exerted by fluids in pore spaces (**fluid pressure**). Other factors which influence metamorphism and rock

Table 2.6 Variation in vertical pressure with depth in crust.

Depth (km)	0	1	2	3	4	5	6	7	8	9	10
Pressure (kbar)	0.001	0.25	0.50	0.75	1.00	1.25	1.50	1.75	2.00	2.25	2.50

deformation are **differential stress**, the difference between maximum and minimum **principal stresses**, and **strain rate**, which is the amount of deformation (or strain) undergone by a rock in a certain time. All these factors are interrelated and they vary from place to place, depending on particular **orogenic** environments.

Total confining pressure is directly related to depth, and it may be thought of as acting vertically, so that vertical pressure is more or less the same as confining pressure. You may have noticed the 'pressure' effect on your eardrums when you were in an aircraft or diving to the bottom of a swimming pool. At any particular depth (or height) the pressure is the same in all directions. Pressure is measured in kilobars (kbar, or thousands of bars). Normal atmospheric pressure at sea level is 1 bar (1000 millibars, mbar). An alternative unit is the Pascal (Pa) where $1\ Pa = 10^{-5}$ bar, although geologists are accustomed to expres-

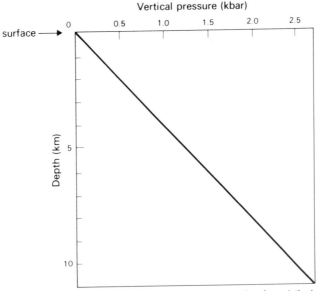

Figure 2.3 Vertical pressure against depth in the crust (i.e. for relatively shallow depths in the continental crust).

sing pressure in kilobars. Plot depth against vertical pressure using the figures in the table above (Table 2.6). Use 0.5 cm paper, and join the points with a smooth curve. Compare your graph with Figure 2.3. It is a straight line over the range of depths shown in Table 2.6, i.e. vertical pressure is directly proportional to depth, until densities begin to change in the lower crust and mantle. The vertical pressure at a depth of 4 km is twice that at 2 km depth. The slope or gradient of the line on Figure 2.3 is one. Figures in Table 2.6 assume that crustal rocks have an average density of 2.5 g cm^{-3}. Values of vertical pressure would be higher for denser rocks. It is now possible for you to add pressure to the temperature–depth graph of Figure 2.1.

What is pore-fluid pressure?

A fluid is a liquid or a gas and it is *mobile*, i.e. it can move through pore spaces in rocks. Important fluids in geology are water and carbon dioxide and to a lesser extent sulphur dioxide and chlorine. These fluids are present in the multitude of pore spaces between grains and in tiny fissures, cracks and veins in almost all rocks, particularly sediments. During deformation and metamorphism, fluids in these pore spaces are heated and compressed. Pore fluids are also under the same pressure as the rocks themselves, owing to depth in the crust. Fluids are capable of exerting their own pressure (**partial pressure**) within pore spaces, which is extremely important during metamorphism. Pore-fluid pressure is also responsible for the spectacular blow-outs that sometimes occur when oil wells are being drilled. Pore-fluid pressure is often very high during certain types of metamorphism.

Stress and strain in the crust

Rocks within the Earth's crust are subjected to stresses (applied forces) acting in all directions. Changes in shape and volume (elongation, flattening, change of angles) resulting from the application of stresses are known as strains (Fig. 2.4). Although stresses in the crust act in all directions, it is possible to simplify matters and consider three principal stresses at right angles to each other. These are referred to as **maximum**, **intermediate** and **minimum** principal stresses, sometimes abbreviated to P_{max}, P_{int} and P_{min} respectively (Fig. 2.5). The difference between the maximum and minimum principal stresses, i.e. $P_{max} - P_{min}$, is known as the stress difference, or differential stress. Actual values of stress

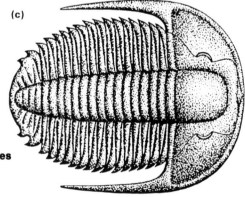

Figure 2.4 Deformed trilobites (*Angelina*) in Welsh slates.
(a) flattened; (b) stretched; (c) undeformed.

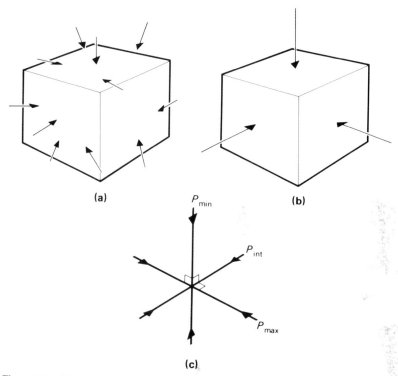

Figure 2.5 Diagrams illustrating principal stresses. (a) Forces acting on the faces of a cube of rock that is being deformed; (b) resolution of these forces perpendicular to faces; (c) stress system referred to three mutually perpendicular axes. P_{min}, minimum principal stress; P_{int}, intermediate principal stress; P_{max}, maximum principal stress. Note that in the crust the axes may be interchanged with one another in particular situations.

difference can sometimes be measured by studying certain features of faults and earthquakes. Differential stress is often relatively low and it averages 250 bars (0.25 kbar) along fault planes. Faults result from brittle deformation in which rocks snap into blocks and move along a plane or narrow zone of crushed rock past each other. Forces have to be quite high to overcome rock strength and friction, and pore-fluid pressure plays a very important role in fault movements in helping to reduce the actual force needed to cause movement.

   When rocks are deformed, or strained, they may fold, break, or store up the strain energy. What actually happens depends on the circumstances, such as temperature, depth, fluid pressure, rock composition, etc. An important factor in rock deformation is the strain rate, which may be thought of as the rate of natural deformation and is measured as a change in the length or shape of a material with time. If pitch or toffee is hit with a hammer, it will shatter like glass because the strain rate is high, i.e. a large force is applied instantaneously, and in this case the material behaves like a **brittle** solid. But if a block of pitch is left on a table, it will very slowly slump and spread out under the effect of gravity and may eventually cover a large area of the table. In this case, the strain rate is low and the pitch behaves like a very sticky (viscous) liquid; it deforms in a **plastic** manner. Rocks which deform plastically remain permanently strained once the stresses are removed. (Contrast this with the **elastic** behaviour of a rubber band, which returns to its original size once the force is removed.) In rock deformation and metamorphism, an important role is played by the phenomenon of **creep**. Creep is time-dependent permanent deformation (strain), resulting in large strains being produced at low continuous stress levels (less than the strength of the material) applied over a long time interval.

The driving force for metamorphic reactions

For all chemical reactions, including those involved in metamorphism, the driving force is the change in **free energy**. Free energy represents the amount of energy that would be released or absorbed during a reversible process (one which can be performed in exactly the reverse direction). Note that it is not the actual quantity of free energy that is important, but the *change* in this quantity. The free energy of a system reaches a minimum when equilibrium has been attained, where a system is considered to be a mineral, a rock or the whole Earth, depending on the scale of the process being investigated. A system is either **open** if its boundaries are not barriers to the movement of material (such as elements or fluid phases like H_2O), or **closed** if its boundaries are or were barriers to the transfer of material across the boundaries. Time and the scale factor are again important: the same system may change from being open to being closed after a certain time interval, or the system may be open to fluids, for example, but closed to element transfer.

Equilibrium in metamorphic reactions

Chemical equilibrium is a concept that may be described as a state of balance reached in a reversible reaction whenever the forward and reverse reactions are proceeding at equal rates. If the system is disturbed by changing one of the factors involved in the equilibrium, such as pressure or temperature, then the equilibrium will shift so as to cancel out the effect of the change. The rate at which equilibrium is attained is important and it depends on pressure, temperature, the presence of fluids, and grain size, among other things.

If a particular set of pressure and temperature conditions is maintained for a sufficiently long period, a rock will continue to recrystallise until a completely new set of minerals (i.e. a new mineral assemblage) forms which is stable under these conditions. In the Earth's crust, a sediment is deposited on the surface and is then buried, heated and recrystallised at some depth below the surface. This is followed by uplift due to erosion of the overlying rocks and cooling until the rock eventually appears at the surface. During metamorphism, the sediment will have followed a specific pressure–temperature **path** through time. Usually the rate at which equilibrium is attained is too slow to allow mineral assemblages to adjust continually to new conditions (e.g. sedimentation and burial rates can be very rapid). The result is that, when a metamorphic rock reaches the surface, it contains a mineral assemblage (e.g. quartz + mica + garnet) which is characteristic of the high pressures and temperatures at some considerable depth in the crust. In such a case the equilibrium has been frozen into the rock; an assemblage such as quartz + mica + garnet cannot form in a rock at the surface. An equilibrium mineral assemblage is one that has attained the lowest energy state under metamorphic conditions.

Crystal growth during metamorphism

New minerals form in metamorphic rocks by the appearance of **nuclei** of a stable mineral phase. Nuclei are minute particles of material, a few hundred atoms large, which act as centres or focal points for growth. Nuclei grow to form crystal grains as more and more material is transferred and attached to the nuclei. The steps involved in **nucleation** (the formation of nuclei) and subsequent **grain growth** are activated by thermal energy. Generally, the higher the temperature, the more nuclei form and the faster the crystals grow.

In crystalline solids, nucleation most often occurs along grain boundaries or within zones of deformation in a rock. The reason is that these are sites where energy is locally higher. Crystals are not perfect at the atomic level, but instead their lattices contain imperfections known as **defects** or **dislocations**. Defects always end at crystal faces (and therefore at grain/grain boundaries in a crystal aggregate) and the energy associated with defects becomes concentrated at grain boundaries.

Crystal growth proceeds from nucleation once a certain critical change in free energy has been exceeded. Material has to be transferred through all the phases involved in a metamorphic reaction by a process known as **diffusion**. Nucleation and crystal growth go on at the same time during a reaction. Diffusion, nucleation and growth are opposed by free energy barriers. They are thermally activated processes which require an input of thermal energy in order to overcome the energy barriers and allow the processes to take place. In other words, high temperatures favour these processes, which is why metamorphic reactions are temperature controlled.

Diffusion during metamorphism

Diffusion is a process by which material in the form of atoms, molecules and ions physically alters position. In solids, atoms jump from site to site in a crystal lattice. Diffusion is controlled by temperature: if sufficient heat is added, energy barriers may be overcome sufficiently to allow atoms to vibrate outside their normal positions. In the crust, gradients of temperature, pressure or chemical concentration exist, with the result that diffusion may show a tendency to cause atoms to move down these gradients, i.e. matter can migrate in one particular direction. Diffusion tends to occur faster along grain boundaries, where there are more defects, than through the body of crystals. As was pointed out in the previous section, the concentration of defects in crystalline material increases with increasing temperature. Atoms of all elements do not diffuse at the same rate. It has been found experimentally that the diffusion of silicon (Si) and aluminium (Al) is almost negligible when compared with other metal ions, at least at the temperatures prevailing during metamorphism.

Recrystallisation during metamorphism

The term 'recrystallisation' in metamorphic petrology is often used to cover two processes: **crystallisation** and **recrystallisation**. Strictly speaking, crystallisation as applied to metamorphic rocks refers to the processes whereby crystals of a new mineral phase form. Crystallisation involves nucleation and grain growth (see p. 29). Recrystallisation may simply involve grain growth, as crystals of the mineral already exist. During metamorphism, crystallisation and recrystallisation may be partial or complete. For example, a quartzite may form from a sandstone by the growth of quartz grains. No recrystallisation is necessary, and the fine details of bedding and cross bedding may be preserved (if present), as in the case of Cambrian quartzites in north-west Scotland. On the other hand, sandstone or chert may be completely recrystallised to quartzite, with the destruction of the original grains and sedimentary structures. In the case of garnet–mica schist, produced from the metamorphism of shale (see p. 75), the new mineral phases garnet and mica grew from the complete reconstitution of all the components in the shale and the crystallisation of the metamorphic minerals. 'Recrystallisation' is used loosely to mean 'crystallisation of new phases' as well as grain growth.

Recrystallisation in metamorphism often takes place together with chemical changes (during metamorphic reactions). The free energy involved in the reactions can itself assist recrystallisation by contributing to the driving force.

Water, even in minute amounts, can affect the rate of recrystallisation. Water has a strong effect on the migration of crystal defects and it causes crystals to become weaker and to recrystallise more readily. Deformation can also assist recrystallisation by speeding up the movement of defects. Recrystallisation is therefore strongly influenced by:

(a) temperature,
(b) chemical changes,
(c) the presence of water, and
(d) deformation.

The overall controlling factor in metamorphism is temperature, which controls the rate of chemical reactions, the mobility of water and the movement and formation of crystal defects.

During recrystallisation, energy is released in two ways. First, **strain energy** that has been locked up in crystals during metamorphism is released. And secondly, the growth of crystals means that the total grain boundary area is reduced as grains grow larger, causing a reduction in the energy associated with grain boundaries. These energy losses form the driving force for recrystallisation. In a sense, recrystallisation causes crystal aggregates to 'relax' and adopt lower energy states in a strain-free condition. Crystals have the lowest possible free energy, so that solids attempt to remain crystalline when they are being acted on by forces (stresses) that are trying to deform them. Recrystallisation (in the strict sense) is possible once the temperature reaches half the melting point of a solid in degrees Kelvin (where $^{\circ}K = ^{\circ}C + 273$; temperature in $^{\circ}K$ is known as the absolute temperature). It is not until this temperature is reached that ions can move sufficiently for recrystallisation to take place.

Metamorphism and crustal processes

One of the main aims of studying metamorphic rocks is to deduce the ways in which pressure, temperature and heat flow have varied with time in the crust. By examining metamorphic minerals and the textures and structures of metamorphic rocks, it is possible to build up a history of how a rock evolved from being deposited at the surface, through burial, metamorphism and eventual emergence at the surface again, owing to erosion or thrusting, as a metamorphic rock.

Sedimentary, igneous and metamorphic rocks are commonly very closely associated in **orogenic belts**. An orogenic belt is a major crustal feature forming a long, narrow, sinuous path in the crust and consisting of a complex association of intensely deformed sediments (and sometimes lavas) that have been metamorphosed and intruded by magma. **Orogenies** (mountain-building events) are relatively short-lived in terms of geological time, of the order of 50–200 million years. The

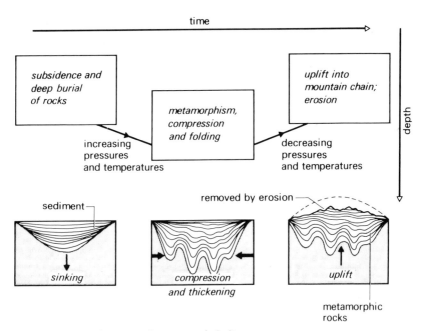

Figure 2.6 Development of an orogenic belt.

geologically young mountain belts of the Rockies, the Alps and the Himalayas are examples of orogenic belts. Mountain belts account for over 10% of the total surface area of the Earth, or 25% of the area of the continents. Orogenic belts have been deeply eroded and they therefore represent cross sections through the deeper parts of the Earth's crust. Orogenic activity involves the accumulation of thick piles of sediments and some lavas at the surface. These piles subside and the sediments become deeply buried, compressed and deformed by folding and are heated up at depth. At the surface, folded sediments are thrown up into high relief, often forming overfolded **nappe** structures, and immediately become subject to the forces of erosion. Vast quantities of material are removed by erosion, and the thickened crust is gradually uplifted. Finally, rocks metamorphosed at depth emerge at the surface, containing new minerals, structures and textures. The processes involved in mountain building and the formation of metamorphic rocks are illustrated schematically in Figure 2.6. The events leading to mountain building belong to the tectonic cycle, which is driven by the Earth's internal heat. By studying the metamorphic minerals in rocks from orogenic belts, it is possible to build up a picture of how pressure, temperature and heat flow have changed in time and space and how rocks have responded to stresses imposed on them during mountain building. We can gain an insight into the way in which physical and chemical conditions change with depth in the crust.

During the operation of the **tectonic cycle**, deeply buried sediments become heated up in two ways. First, sediments contain fragments of crustal rocks which themselves contain radioactive isotopes. These isotopes continue to give out heat as they decay within the sedimentary pile. Secondly, as the sediments sink or are pushed farther down into the crust, they absorb more of the heat rising from deeper within the Earth. Eventually the sedimentary pile becomes thick enough to allow lateral compression and folding to take place. These compressive forces, together with the self-heat (from radioactivity) and internal heat cause rocks to be metamorphosed. The Earth's crust is locally thickened in a vertical sense by lateral compression of sediments. Conversely, the crust is shortened in a horizontal sense in orogenic belts. In addition, igneous rocks may have been intruded directly from the upper mantle into the thick sediments at the base of the orogenic belt. Conditions of pressure and temperature at those depths are such that the magmas may crystallise with metamorphic mineral assemblages. The distinction between igneous and metamorphic rocks then becomes less clear. Intrusion of thick sheets of magmatic rocks is another possible way in which the crust can be thickened in orogenic belts.

Igneous intrusions play a part in causing local metamorphism of other rocks by adding heat and sometimes hot fluids to them. Metamorphic effects around intrusions decrease rapidly away from the igneous body as heat is dissipated (Fig. 2.7, see also p. 46). It is found that granitic intrusions cause more pronounced and more widespread metamorphic effects than do gabbroic and other basic intrusions, although the latter are at a much higher temperature. In other words, aureoles around granites are wider than around gabbros. One of the main reasons is that granitic magmas are 'wet' relative to basic magmas; water and other hot, active fluids transport heat and assist crystallisation and recrystallisation. Some granites in orogenic belts, which were intruded near the base of a thick sedimentary pile, may not have caused noticeable metamorphic effects in the surrounding rocks, the latter having been at the elevated temperatures caused by deep burial. Rocks formed deep within orogenic belts may also be brought to or near the surface by **overthrusting**. **Thrusts** or **overthrusts** are low-angled displacement surfaces along which blocks of crustal rock have been moved for some distance horizontally (of the order of 5–50 km, sometimes more). The tectonic unit overlying a thrust is called a **thrust sheet**. Thrusts occur in the upper and outer parts of orogenic belts. Grinding, crushing, shearing and frictional heat in thrust zones can lead to the formation of mylo-

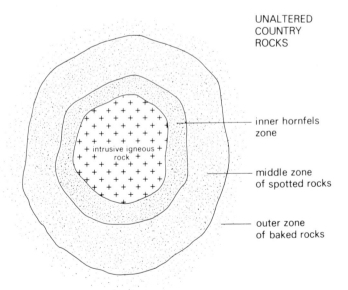

UNALTERED
COUNTRY
ROCKS

inner hornfels
zone

intrusive igneous rock

middle zone
of spotted rocks

outer zone
of baked rocks

Figure 2.7   Contact aureole around an igneous intrusion.

nites, which are fine-grained recrystallised rocks with a banded appearance and showing signs of intense deformation. In many thrust zones, water has played a significant role in the transport of the thrust sheets and in the recrystallisation of the metamorphic rocks within the thrust zone. Some of the possible mechanisms of thrusting and the resultant metamorphic rock products are discussed further in Chapter 3.

Plate tectonics and metamorphic rocks

Plate tectonics theory considers that the Earth's lithosphere (crust and part of the upper mantle) is composed of a mosaic of shells or rigid plates 50–150 km thick (Fig. 2.8). These lithospheric plates are situated above the **asthenosphere**, which in contrast to the solid lithosphere is a dense, viscous layer within the upper mantle which is capable of moving slowly and deforming in a plastic manner. The hypothesis of sea-floor spreading assumes that new lithosphere is being created continuously at ocean rises (**mid-ocean ridges**) by the intrusion and extrusion of magma derived by **partial melting** of the asthenosphere. New lithosphere spreads laterally away from mid-ocean ridges as more material is added there, and eventually the lithosphere (mainly oceanic) is returned to the asthenosphere by being consumed in **subduction zones** (Fig. 2.9). The study of plate boundaries and plate interactions is known as plate tectonics.

Plate tectonics proposes that mountain building (or orogenesis) takes place where two plates converge or collide. Plate convergence is dealt with further in Chapter 4. Meanwhile it is important to be aware that there are several different kinds of plate convergence, each with its own characteristic tectonic features. A mountain belt such as the Himalayas (Fig. 2.10) is thought to have been formed by a continent/continent collision when the Indian continent collided with the Eurasian plate. In a continent/continent collision (illustrated schematically in Fig. 2.11) the intervening ocean basin closes as the two continental plates converge and the sediments in the seas around the continents and in the ocean are compressed together. When collision eventually occurs, the buoyancy of the relatively light continents largely prevents them from being subducted down into the mantle. Instead, the crust becomes vertically thickened as the continental masses are compressed and laterally shortened. The resistance to subduction causes large nappe folds and thrust faults to form. Ensuing uplift gives rise to a mountain chain. Temperature and pressure increase in the thickened crust; partial melting may occur and rocks are metamorphosed and intruded by granite

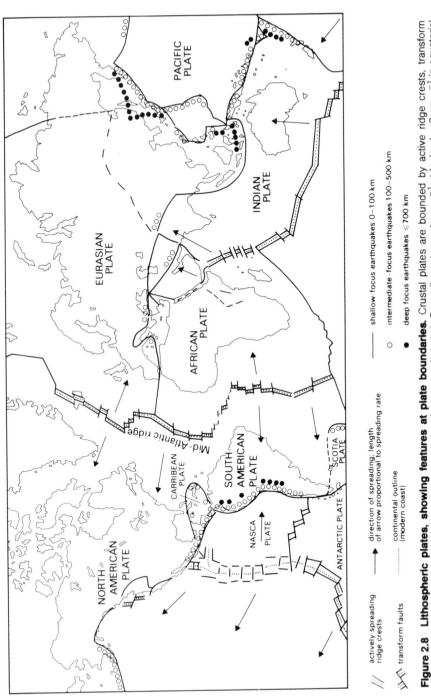

Figure 2.8 Lithospheric plates, showing features at plate boundaries. Crustal plates are bounded by active ridge crests, transform faults, trench systems and zones of compression (young fold mountain belts). Spreading rates: ~1 cm y⁻¹ at Iceland, ~9 cm y⁻¹ in equatorial Pacific Ocean.

/// actively spreading ridge crests

⟨⟨⟨ transform faults

→ direction of spreading; length of arrow proportional to spreading rate

········· continental outline (modern coast)

— shallow-focus earthquakes 0–100 km

○ intermediate-focus earthquakes 100–500 km

● deep focus earthquakes ⩽700 km

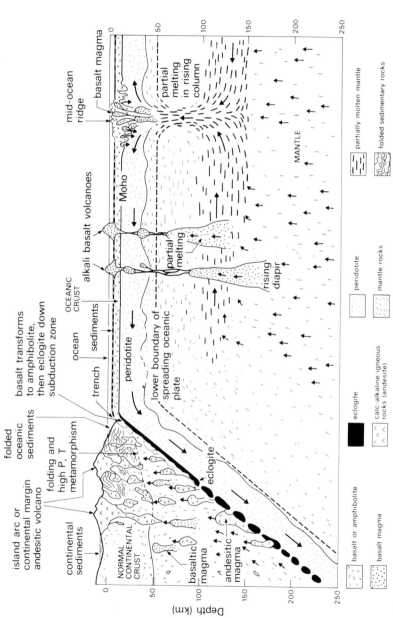

Figure 2.9 Tectonic plate margins: schematic section through a mid-oceanic ridge (constructive margin) and a subduction zone (destructive).

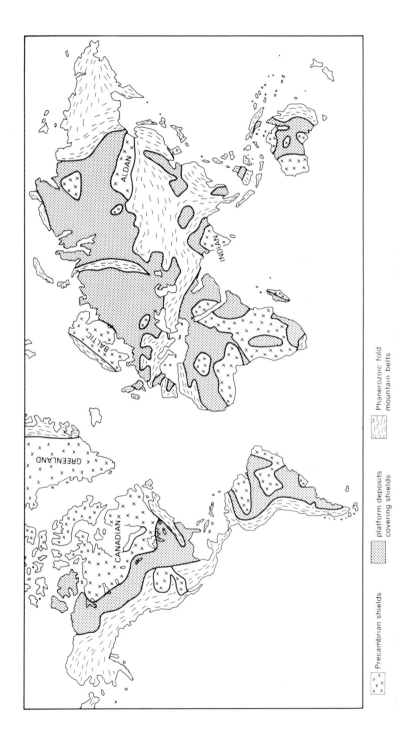

Figure 2.10 Precambrian shields, platform sediments and Phanerozoic fold mountain belts.

Precambrian shields

platform deposits covering shields

Phanerozoic fold mountain belts

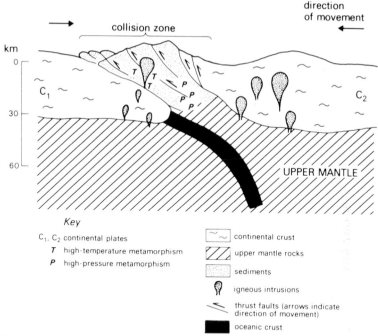

Figure 2.11   A continent/continent plate collision zone.

plutons. The collision zone is marked by a boundary known as a **suture** or suture zone where the two formerly independent continents have become welded together. Suture zones are often interpreted as marking the sites of former oceans that closed during plate convergence. Examples of major sutures are found in the north Himalayas and down the centre of the Ural mountain chain in central USSR.

The energy source for plate movements is the Earth's internal heat which 'drives' the lithospheric plates and controls mountain building and metamorphism. This is discussed in greater detail in Chapter 4.

Metamorphic grades, zones and facies

Metamorphic grade is a term used to give a relative measure of the intensity of metamorphism in a particular area. Grade of metamorphism is often equated with temperature, i.e. low metamorphic grades occur at low temperatures, forming low-grade rocks, and high grades occur at relatively high temperatures. Many low-grade metamorphic rocks derived from shales and mudstones (initially wet, fine-grained sediments) contain hydrated minerals, such as chlorite and muscovite. Several of the reactions that take place with increasing metamorphic grade within a sequence of progressive metamorphism (see p. 48) involve dehydration of these minerals, i.e. their combined water is driven off. The new, high-grade mineral assemblages are stable at high temperatures and are anhydrous. It is also possible to use the term 'grade' to indicate relative intensity of metamorphism at constant temperature but progressively increasing pressure.

A progressive metamorphic sequence in an area may be subdivided in the field into **metamorphic zones** or zones of different metamorphic grades. A metamorphic zone is characterised by the appearance of a distinctive **index mineral**. Index minerals mark definite stages (i.e. metamorphic zones) of increasing grade. Lines on a map that separate individual metamorphic zones are referred to a **isograds** or lines of equal grade. Isograds are put on a map whenever the first appearance of the index mineral of a particular zone is recognised. For example, the chlorite zone in the south-east Scottish Highlands (see pp. 71–2 & Fig. 3.18) contains the index mineral chlorite. The next highest grade in these particular rocks is shown by the biotite zone, the index mineral of the zone being of course biotite. The start of the biotite zone is marked by the biotite isograd which separates the chlorite and biotite zones on the map.

One of the drawbacks about using metamorphic zones is that the growth of index minerals is largely chemically controlled. For example, a sandstone containing 100% quartz can never develop biotite as an index mineral, no matter what the grade is: the ingredients for making biotite are simply not present in a sandstone. It often turns out that complete mineral assemblages have to be used to determine metamorphic grade, rather than single minerals. Remember that the mineral assemblage developed in a metamorphic rock depends on the chemical composition of the original rock, together with that of any fluids present, and the pressure–temperature conditions. In the example of the Scottish Highlands referred to above, metamorphic zones were originally based on index minerals in metamorphosed shales and mudstones because the initial composition of these sediments was such that they were very reactive. Another factor in this regard is the fine-grained nature of the sediments. Metamorphic minerals grew readily in them, so that they are more useful at indicating metamorphic grade than, for example, sandstones would be.

A **metamorphic facies** is defined as a set or collection of metamorphic mineral assemblages, repeatedly associated in time and space so that there is a constant relationship between mineral assemblage and rock composition. The term 'metamorphic facies' is a mineralogical one, incorporating several mineral assemblages or rock types which formed under the same *broad* conditions of temperature and pressure. This implies that rocks of the same chemical composition have the same mineral assemblage if they belong to the same metamorphic facies. The concept of metamorphic facies has been used to give a broad classification of the pressure–temperature conditions of metamorphism, but it must be emphasised that it was introduced to deal with mineral assemblages, not conditions or processes (Fig. 2.12). As in the case of metamorphic zones, the facies classification can only be used successfully if rocks of suitable composition are present. A further disadvantage of the facies scheme is that it does not readily allow for variations in the composition of fluids or in fluid partial pressures (see p. 25). Commonly used facies (described further in Ch. 3) apply to situations where water is the only fluid and where the partial pressure of water is assumed to have been equal to the total pressure operating during metamorphism. Such conditions are quite special and do not constitute the most general case. The difficulties involved in applying the metamorphic facies concept to actual rock associations have led to its being largely abandoned

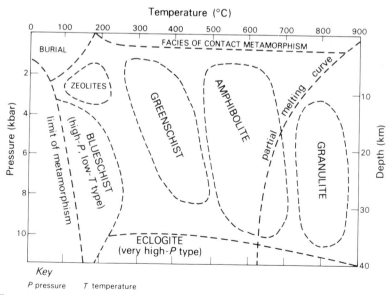

Figure 2.12 Pressure–temperature diagram showing locations of the various facies of regional metamorphism.

in the last few years. However, if it is recognised that the pressure–temperature conditions implied by a certain facies are extremely broad, then the use of a metamorphic facies scheme in very general mapping of an extensive region still has some merit and can form a base for more detailed research work.

Classifying metamorphic processes

As shown above, the controlling factors of metamorphism, i.e. load pressure, temperature, strain and vapour partial pressures, vary continuously in the crust. From this it is to be expected that metamorphism is itself a **continuum** process, by which is meant that the possible permutations and combinations of controlling factors lead to every gradation in the types of metamorphism. For convenience, this continuum can be broken down into end members. The traditional subdivisions of metamorphism are thermal (contact), dynamic and regional, but this classification has several drawbacks in that it fails to take account of the considerable overlap in the three types. For example, some dynamic metamorphic rocks in thrust zones contain mineral assemblages that also occur in regional metamorphic rocks. Or, in the case of some granites which were intruded into crustal rocks with great force, the mineral assemblages in the contact metamorphic rocks in the aureole may be identical to those found in regional metamorphic rocks. In the latter case, high strain has led to unusual contact metamorphic assemblages. One further disadvantage of the classical scheme is that the field of regional metamorphism is much too wide. The classical scheme is based on pressure and temperature only and it makes no allowance for strain, fluid composition or vapour partial pressures. Regional metamorphism covers a large range of pressures and temperatures. These problems have already been alluded to in Chapter 1, where (p. 3) it was pointed out that a more satisfactory subdivision of metamorphism is based on all the variables, giving us such end members as high temperature, low pressure, low strain, variable vapour pressure metamorphism, which is equivalent to thermal metamorphism. The broad field of regional metamorphism can then be subdivided more satisfactorily into subfields that correspond with actual crustal conditions in various tectonic environments.

Summary

A principal cause of metamorphism is the Earth's heat, which is derived from the decay of radioactive elements that are concentrated in the crust, together with heat transferred upwards from the mantle into the base of the crust. Heat transfer in the solid lithosphere is mainly by conduction, and in the upper mantle is by convection in a viscous semi-solid. Heat flow varies in different geological provinces, being greatest in active oceanic volcanic belts and least in old, stable continental platforms.

The other factors responsible for metamorphism are pressure, which increases with depth, strain and vapour partial pressures (mainly H_2O and CO_2).

Metamorphic reactions are driven by the change in the chemical free energy of a system. Reactions take place until equilibrium is achieved between the phases of a system at particular pressure and temperature conditions, with the formation of metamorphic mineral assemblages characteristic of the conditions. Reaction rates are controlled by rock chemistry, grain size, the presence and composition of fluids, temperature and strain.

Metamorphism takes place in the solid state (because crystals have the lowest free energy state) with the nucleation and subsequent grain growth of new and pre-existing mineral phases. Material is added to allow grain growth by solid state diffusion, mostly along grain boundaries. Recrystallisation takes place at high temperatures and is driven by released strain energy.

Metamorphic processes are mainly restricted to the Earth's continental crust and occur in orogenic belts, where igneous, sedimentary and metamorphic rocks are closely associated together. Orogenic belts contain folded and metamorphosed sedimentary rocks, often intruded by magmatic rocks in their deeper parts. Orogenic belts originate when lithospheric plates collide. The continental crust in collision zones is thickened, compressed and folded. Pressure, temperature and deformation increase, causing rock metamorphism to occur.

A sequence of progressive metamorphic grades may be conveniently subdivided into metamorphic zones characterised by distinctive index minerals. Metamorphic grades and zones depend for their recognition on original rock compositions.

A metamorphic facies is a set of mineral assemblages (rock types) which formed under the same broad pressure–temperature conditions. Mineral assemblages are strongly dependent on original rock compositions.

Since the factors controlling metamorphism vary continuously, metamorphism is a continuum process. For convenience, the continuum may be broken down into end members. The classic subdivisions of metamorphism are thermal (contact), dynamic and regional, which are respectively high-temperature–low-pressure, low-strain metamorphism; high-strain, variable-pressure, variable-temperature metamorphism; and high-temperature–high-pressure, variable strain metamorphism.

Exercises

1   Why do many metamorphic rocks show parallel orientation of their mineral grains?
2   How is it possible to gain some knowledge concerning the temperature inside the crust?
3   List some uses of radioactive isotopes (e.g. in the fields of medicine, energy, geology).
4   Obtain some water, treacle, glycerine and pitch. Place a ball-bearing on the surface of a beaker filled with each of these materials and note the time taken for the ball-bearing to fall through the same distance in each substance. Which is the most viscous and which the least?
5   What effect, if any, do you think temperature might have on the experiment outlined above?
6   Place an equal weight on equal lengths of steel wire, copper wire and rubber of the same thickness. Note how much the materials increase in length in each case. If you divide the weight by the change in length you will obtain a figure which is a specific constant for each of these materials. It is the modulus of elasticity, or the stress : strain ratio.
7   Using Table 2.4, make a graph of heat flow against age for the oceanic crust. Compare it with Figure 2.2. Is there any similarity? Why?

3 Metamorphic terrains I

The aim of this and the next chapter is to present some case studies of areas containing metamorphic rocks from the points of view of field relations and metamorphic processes. The classical divisions of contact, dynamic and regional metamorphism will be used, together with their equivalents based on pressure, temperature, strain and fluid partial pressures (see Ch. 2).

Contact metamorphism

At shallow depths in the crust, heat sources responsible for contact metamorphism are bodies of hot magma (i.e. igneous intrusions) which locally raise the temperature of crustal rocks. The resulting thermal effects are restricted to the contact zones of the intrusions with the country rocks they intrude. Many intrusions will release hot fluids into the surrounding country rocks as they cool, and these fluids can also play a role in the formation of new minerals. Heat is transmitted to the country rocks by conduction, as pointed out on page 20. The most important features of an igneous intrusion in determining the thermal metamorphic effects on the country rocks are the size of the intrusion and its initial temperature. The initial temperature in turn is controlled by the type of intrusion: basic magmas are hotter than acid magmas. Igneous intrusions range in size from massive batholiths down to such minor intrusions as plugs, sills and dykes. A batholith would give rise to metamorphic effects much farther away from its margins than would a dyke. A worked example should make this clear. Use the information in Table 3.1 to plot a graph of the temperature of country rocks against distance away from the contact of an intrusion. You will obtain three curves for different types of magma in the intrusions. The figures are for plutons of 5 km diameter, intruded to a depth of 5 km below the surface, where the temperature of the country rocks before intrusion was around 150 °C. Suggested scales: 4 cm horizontally ≡ 1 km, 1 cm vertically ≡ 100 °C. Put in the country rock temperature, and compare your graph with Figure 3.1. An extra curve has been added to Figure 3.1, showing the decrease in temperature away from a smaller pluton (1 km

Table 3.1 Temperatures of magmas and country rocks away from igneous intrusions (5 km diameter, 5 km deep).

Magma type	Temperature of intrusion (°C)	Temp. at contact	Temp. away from intrusion		
			0.5 km	1.0 km	2.5 km
gabbro	1200	875	775	700	550
syenite	900	700	625	550	450
granite	800	650	575	500	425

in diameter, as opposed to 5 km). Note carefully the shapes of the four curves: they are steep at first and they gradually 'tail off'. This particular shape of graph will be referred to again.

Rocks adjacent to an igneous intrusion are heated and, if the body of magma is large enough, the rise in temperature of the country rocks will last long enough to allow mineral reactions to take place. Rocks in contact with thin dykes and sills do not experience great changes and are simply baked and hardened, with possibly some of the cement in

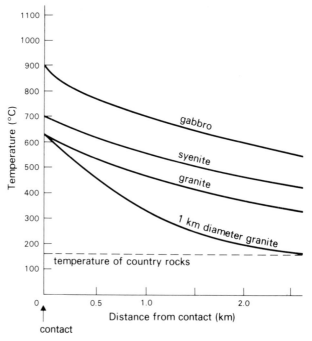

Figure 3.1 Temperature against distance from igneous contacts.

sedimentary rocks being recrystallised so that grains are welded together. On the other hand, large plutons give rise to a **contact aureole** within which the country rocks are thermally metamorphosed. Several **zones** of increasing temperature may be recognised in contact aureoles, as one approaches the pluton. For an intrusion of, say, 5 km in diameter the country rocks will stay very hot for several tens of thousands of years, long enough for chemical reactions to continue to completion, thereby allowing equilibrium (p. 9) between adjacent minerals to be achieved.

Contact metamorphism of pelitic rocks. Pelitic rocks are usually defined to be metamorphosed argillaceous sediments (shales and mudstones), although some authors use the term to mean non-metamorphosed rocks as well. The major constituents of argillaceous sediments are mica, clay minerals, quartz, iron ores, carbon compounds and sometimes carbonates. Shales and mudstones are very fine grained and they contain a great variety of mineral grains, which are the breakdown products of feldspar, mica, pyroxene, olivine, iron ore and animal and plant matter, together with quartz, which is stable. Many of the grains are hydrated, i.e. they contain water in their structure. This variety means that there is an abundance of chemical elements, so allowing for the possibility that a great number of different minerals can potentially form from a mudstone or shale parent during metamorphism. The 'ingredients' of a typical argillaceous sediment are set out in Table 3.2. Contrast this list with the contents of sandstone : quartz (SiO_2). When a sandstone is metamorphosed, nothing but quartz can grow, i.e.

$$\text{sandstone} \xrightarrow[\text{pressure}]{\text{heat and/or}} \text{quartzite}$$

The texture of a quartzite is different from that of a sandstone, but not the composition.

Table 3.2 Main constituents of argillaceous sediments.

silica
micas ⎱
clays ⎰ rich in alumina
iron oxides, hydroxides and sulphides
carbonates, chlorides, sulphates
carbon (graphite, plant remains)
water, carbon dioxide, sulphur, chlorine

The fact that the particles in argillaceous sediments are very small means that each grain has a large surface area for its size, and since chemical reactions during metamorphism largely take place at grain boundaries, reactions can proceed quite fast between all these 'ingredients', which are in close contact and are in the presence of fluids, such as water. Shales and mudstones are most sensitive to the effects of heat, and new minerals grow at progressively higher temperatures (Fig. 3.2). Because such a great variety of new minerals can grow during the metamorphism of argillaceous rocks, these rocks are useful for dividing up the pressure–temperature space of metamorphism. In a sandstone on the other hand, the only metamorphic changes are textural, not mineralogical. But since the textural changes in a sandstone are less temperature sensitive than the mineralogical changes in argillaceous rocks, sandstones are not much good as indicators of metamorphic grade.

An often quoted example of a contact metamorphic aureole in pelitic rocks is the Skiddaw aureole surrounding a granite of Devonian age that has intruded slates (see p. 71) of Ordovician age in the English Lake District. The granite batholith is an oval-shaped dome, measuring some 10×6 km with a wide aureole (Fig. 3.3). From the width of the aureole, it would appear that the roof of the dome is close to the present land surface. The country rocks outside the aureole are muscovite–chlorite slates with a strong directional fabric (slaty cleavage, see p. 71); the rocks were already deformed and metamorphosed by low-pressure–low temperature (regional) metamorphism before the intrusion of the granite. The metamorphic zones in the Skiddaw aureole form a progressive metamorphic sequence indicating increasing temperature inwards from the country rocks to the contact with the igneous mass. The metamorphic zones are:

unaltered country rocks (Skiddaw Slates)

steadily | outer zone of spotted slates
increasing | middle zone of andalusite slates
temperature ↓ inner zone of hornfels

igneous rock (Skiddaw granite)

In the zone of **spotted slates**, the grain size is slightly coarser than in the country rocks, and small dark spots are visible in the rock. The distinctive marks in a spotted rock result from finely disseminated organic matter or iron ore dust crystallising and coalescing around centres of crystallisation (nuclei, see p. 29) as round or oval spots, clots and patches. In the middle zone, porphyroblasts of andalusite and

(a)

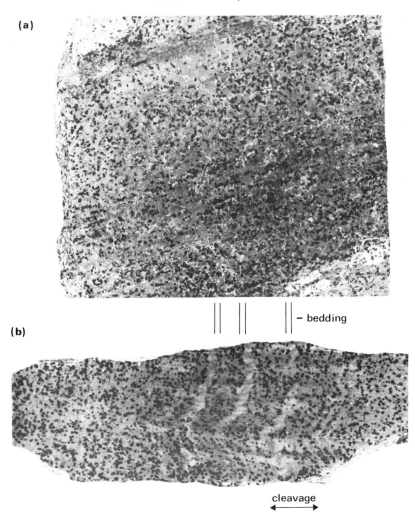

– bedding

(b)

cleavage

Figure 3.2 Hand specimen of spotted slate. Spots appear as dark, circular clots, about 1 mm in diameter. (a) view of cleavage surface, showing irregular distribution of spots; (b) at right angles to (a), showing cleavage (horizontal, indistinct) and bedding (vertical and folded), with spots cutting across cleavage and partly controlled by chemistry of individual beds.

cordierite appear. Andalusite is an aluminium silicate (Al_2SiO_5) polymorph, the third member of the 'family' referred to on page 11. Andalusite crystals are usually conspicuous, as they are prismatic and have a square cross section and light colour. Impurities are present in andalusite at low metamorphic grades and are commonly arranged in

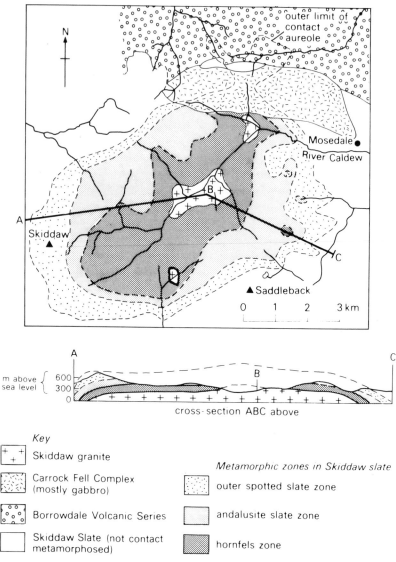

Figure 3.3   Skiddaw aureole, Lake District.

Key

(+ +) Skiddaw granite

(≈≈) Carrock Fell Complex (mostly gabbro)

(∘∘) Borrowdale Volcanic Series

(☐) Skiddaw Slate (not contact metamorphosed)

Metamorphic zones in Skiddaw slate

(∵) outer spotted slate zone

(☐) andalusite slate zone

(▓) hornfels zone

the shape of a cross, giving the variety of andalusite known as **chiastolite** (Fig. 3.4). Impurities or **inclusions** are absent at higher grades as they are either expelled or absorbed into the crystal lattice of andalusite at higher temperatures.

Closer to the igneous intrusion, in the inner contact zone of the

Figure 3.4   Chiastolite, showing cross-shaped inclusion pattern.

metamorphic aureole, the original slate has been completely recrystallised to a hard, splintery, fine- to medium-grained rock called a hornfels.
This texture results from quartz grains growing slightly larger and
becoming firmly welded together. Biotite, cordierite and quartz are the
commonest minerals in medium-grade hornfelses. These rocks often
have a vitreous or glassy lustre due to the quartz having been recrystallised. In the inner zone, the grain size of the rock is again larger and the
hornfels is more massive than the original slate due to the cleavage
being partly obliterated during recrystallisation. This happens because
quartz grains grow across the cleavage surfaces in a random fashion. The
texture of the hornfels is **granoblastic**, i.e. the quartz grains are
equidimensional and form an interlocking mosaic (Fig. 3.5). Granoblastic textures are often an indication that the minerals have reached a state
of equilibrium.

In addition to textural changes, there are mineralogical changes in
the rocks of the Skiddaw aureole. The mineral assemblage of the Skiddaw Slates is:

chlorite + clay minerals + quartz

Biotite is the first new mineral to grow, followed by andalusite and
cordierite, giving the following metamorphic mineral assemblages in the

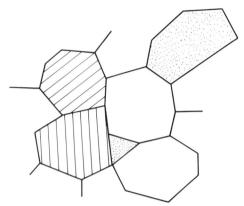

Figure 3.5 Granoblastic texture. Nearly even-grained; crystals frequently meet at 120° angles.

aureole rocks:

biotite + chlorite + clay minerals + quartz
(a low-temperature assemblage)

cordierite + andalusite + muscovite + biotite + quartz
(a high-temperature assemblage)

Chlorite has disappeared in the high-temperature assemblage because it has been replaced by the new minerals, i.e. the constituents of chlorite have been incorporated into other minerals during chemical reactions.

Contact metamorphism of carbonate rocks. Typical carbonate sediments are calcite limestone, dolomite limestone (or dolostone) and impure (muddy) calcareous shales. Calcite is calcium carbonate ($CaCO_3$) and dolomite is calcium–magnesium carbonate, whose chemical formula is $CaMg(CO_3)_2$. The major components of carbonate rocks are set out in Table 3.3.

Table 3.3 Main components of carbonate sediments.

Rock type	Constituents
calcite limestone	calcium carbonate
dolomite limestone	calcium-magnesium carbonate
muddy lime shale	calcium(-magnesium) carbonate, silica, clay minerals (alumina), carbon, various sulphides

Carbonate rocks form various kinds of marbles and **skarns** when thermally altered. Calcite limestone will form an even-grained white marble, in which calcite crystals are welded together. Likewise, dolomite alters to dolomite marble, but a complication arises because other minerals may grow due to dolomite being calcium–magnesium carbonate, which is more complex than calcite. The chemical reaction that takes place when dolomite is thermally metamorphosed is represented by the following equation:

$$CaMg(CO_3)_2 \longrightarrow CaCO_3 + MgO + CO_2$$

dolomite　　　　　　　calcite　　periclase　carbon dioxide

In the case of impure carbonates, silica in the form of sand grains and clay minerals may also be present in addition to calcite or dolomite. The equation for a relatively simple metamorphic reaction involving two of the components in an impure limestone is:

$$CaCO_3 + SiO_2 \longrightarrow CaSiO_3 + CO_2$$

calcite　　quartz　　　wollastonite　carbon dioxide

A new mineral, wollastonite, forms and carbon dioxide gas is released as a fluid phase, which may find its way out of the system through pore spaces and along grain boundaries in the rock. Compare this with the release of water (dehydration) during the metamorphism of shales, which was referred to previously (p. 11, p. 40). The process involving loss of carbon dioxide is referred to as decarbonation.

The mineral garnet (calcium–aluminium silicate) often grows in marbles which were originally calcareous shales, and may form quite large red crystals in a whitish mosaic of calcite, sometimes streaked green with epidote.

Do not worry about the new mineral names (periclase, wollastonite and epidote) which have been introduced. The important point to be aware of is that chemical reactions take place due to the input of heat, to produce mineral assemblages which differ from those of the original sediments. The resulting metamorphic mineral assemblages are determined as much by the composition of the original rocks as by the conditions of metamorphism.

An example of a contact aureole in carbonate rocks is that surrounding the Beinn an Dubhaich granite in the south of the Isle of Skye in the Inner Hebrides of Scotland (Fig. 3.6). This granite, which is part of a complex of Tertiary age igneous intrusions, has intruded a Cambrian dolomitic limestone containing chert (SiO_2) nodules. At the contact with

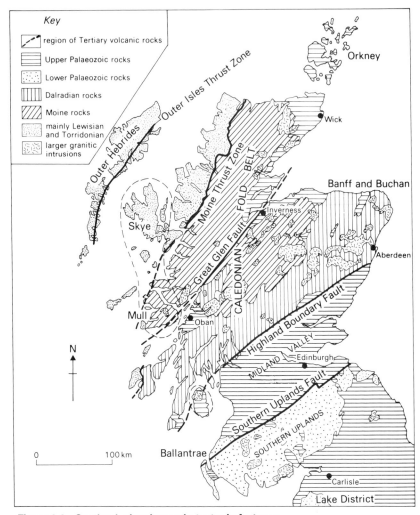

Figure 3.6 Scotland, showing main tectonic features.

the granite, the dolomite has been altered to give the assemblage:

$$\text{calcite (CaCO}_3) + \text{periclase (MgO)}$$

The equation for this reaction is given on page 53. Reactions between silica of the chert and dolomite of the limestone have produced a sequence of new minerals. Because of the original nature of the chert nodules, the new minerals are often in the form of **reaction rims** surrounding chert cores. The sequence of minerals formed with increasing metamorphic grade around the nodules is:

talc → amphibole → pyroxene → olivine → periclase → wollastonite
(low grade)   (high grade)

Examining this sequence closely, we find that the minerals talc and amphibole that formed at low grade are hydrous, i.e. water must have been present to allow these minerals to form from silica and dolomite. The minerals formed at higher grades, though, are **anhydrous**, indicating that the water has been driven off during metamorphism. In the case of the Beinn an Dubhaich aureole we have an example of progressive dehydration and decarbonation with increasing grade (increasing temperature).

Dynamic metamorphic rocks

Dynamic metamorphic rocks, like those of contact (thermal) metamorphism, are of local occurrence. They are restricted to narrow zones adjacent to faults and thrusts. The high shear stress (p. 59) in fault zones leads to crushing of wall rocks along the fault. Temperatures may be raised by the frictional heat generated within the fault zone, but there is no regional heating of the country rocks. High shear stresses may be short-lived or they may persist for millions of years, as in the case of the San Andreas Fault in California and the Moine Thrust Zone and Great Glen Fault in northern Scotland (Fig. 3.6). Dynamic metamorphism involves high pressure, high strain, high fluid partial pressure and variable temperature. In many instances, water plays a fundamentally important role in metamorphic processes within fault and thrust zones.

Crushed rocks in fault zones are known as breccia (or fault breccia). These rocks have angular fragments of the country rock set in a matrix of crushed, powdered or milled rock, cemented by quartz or calcite (Fig. 3.7). Fluids move relatively easily in fault zones along grain boundaries and through pores, cracks and fissures. In so doing, they are able to transport large amounts of silica, carbonates and other materials. Breccias are not recrystallised and thus do not really fall within our definition of metamorphic rocks.

As an example of dynamic metamorphism, the rocks and structures found in the Outer Isles Thrust Zone in the Outer Hebrides of Scotland (Figs. 3.6 & 8) are described and interpreted in terms of metamorphic processes.

Figure 3.7   Fault breccia. Hand specimen; angular rock fragments cemented by calcite.

The Outer Isles Thrust is a major fault formed late in the **Caledonian orogeny** (p. 71), which runs along the eastern coastline of the Outer Hebrides. This structure cuts across crystalline gneisses (p. 77) of the Lewisian Gneiss Complex (p. 83), of biotite–hornblende–quartz–feldspar composition. The thrust zone is up to 30 km wide and it consists of belts of breccia, crushed rock, quartz mylonite and foliated mica-rich mylonite orientated parallel to the thrust (Fig. 3.9). Beneath the base of the main thrust are a number of parallel minor thrusts containing **pseudotachylyte**, which increase in number towards the thrust base (Fig. 3.10). Pseudotachylyte is a black, glassy fault rock with the composition of an acid igneous rock, which is thought to have formed by the melting of the gneiss rocks. In the field, pseudotachylyte usually occurs as small, narrow dykes, veins and networks cutting across the gneiss in an irregular fashion.

The very high temperatures (800 °C at least) necessary to melt gneiss would have resulted from the frictional heat generated by the rapid sliding of one block of gneiss over another, along the thrust fault. Pseudotachylyte is an intrusive fault rock in a sense, and it seems likely that some kind of fluid phase played an important part in its formation.

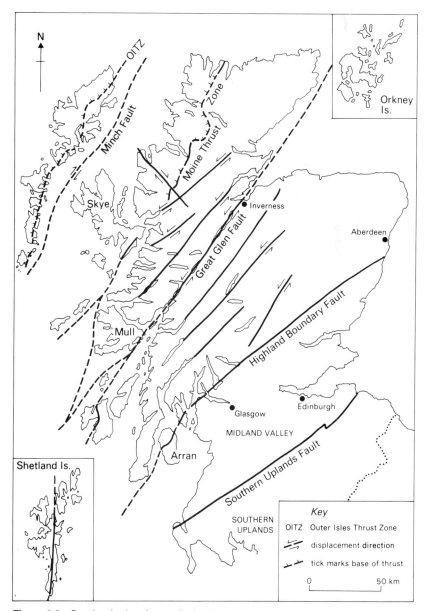

Figure 3.8   Scotland, showing main fault and thrust zones.

Key

OITZ   Outer Isles Thrust Zone

displacement direction

tick marks base of thrust

0 _____ 50 km

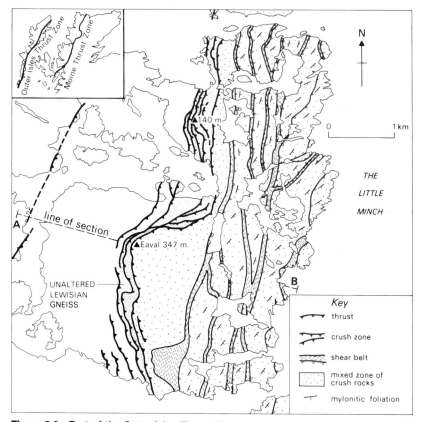

Figure 3.9 Part of the Outer Isles Thrust Zone.

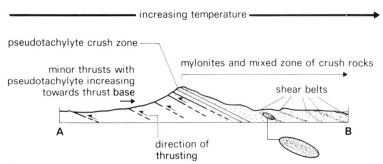

Figure 3.10 Section across part of the area of Figure 3.9, showing minor thrusts, pseudotachylyte and mylonite zones.

Frictional heat and the explosive release of stored-up strain energy and its conversion to heat, together with abundant gas, would give rise to this type of fault rock with the intrusive features evident in the field.

Above the base of the thrust, a network of mylonite belts up to 50 m thick penetrates and criss-crosses a mixed zone of crushed gneisses (breccias). The mylonite belts contain a **schistosity** (p. 75) parallel to their margins. They are termed **shear belts** because they originate due to the action of **shearing stress**. A shearing stress is a force that tends to deform a body by translating one part of it relative to another (contrast this with compressive and tensile stresses, Fig. 3.11). Rocks in the shear belts referred to here have responded to shearing stress by deforming in a **ductile** manner. The ductile behaviour of rocks is controlled by temperature and strain rate (p. 27). At high temperatures and pressures and low strain rates, rocks are more likely to behave in a ductile manner. By contrast, the lower the temperature and pressure and the higher the strain rate, the more likely a particular rock is to behave in a brittle manner (p. 28). Brittle behaviour involves faulting, fracturing and

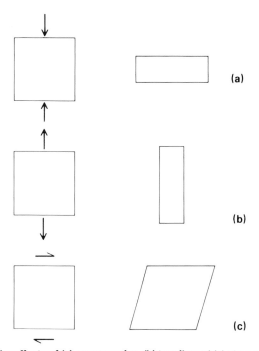

Figure 3.11   The effects of (a) compressive, (b) tensile and (c) shearing stresses.
The squares on the left are strained to give the shapes on the right in each case.

grinding of grains, whereas ductile behaviour involves the deformation
of individual grains by slipping along certain crystal planes, by twinning
and by processes involving diffusion (p. 30). Higher temperatures and
lower strain rates favour crystal slip and atomic diffusion (i.e. these are
thermally activated processes).

In the Outer Hebrides Thrust Zone the rock types and the fabrics
they contain may be separated into two groups, reflecting two distinct
processes and patterns of rock behaviour in the crust during the formation of the thrust. Breccia and pseudotachylyte possess random fabrics
and they formed owing to frictional effects on rocks which behaved
elastically during deformation. A rock behaves elastically if it regains
its original size, shape and volume once it is unloaded, i.e. the (tempor-
ary) strain disappears when the stress is removed. If the stress applied to
the rock is greater than the rock's strength, then it will break and the
deformation is brittle. Rocks usually behave elastically in the upper
crust (1–10 km depth approximately). Below a certain depth, around
10–15 km, rocks begin to behave plastically, and deformation becomes
permanent, i.e. a rock will not revert to its original shape once the stress
responsible for deformation is removed. In the Outer Isles Thrust Zone,
mylonites with directional fabrics formed in shear belts within which the

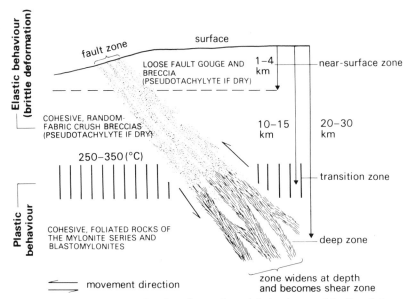

**Figure 3.12   A fault zone, showing change in rock behaviour and fault rock types
with increasing depth.**

fault rocks behaved plastically. The situation is summarised diagrammatically in Figure 3.12.

The transition from elastic to plastic behaviour is affected by temperature and the availability of water in the fault zone. In the elastic zone (Fig. 3.12), material is broken down in crush zones and it becomes progressively smaller in grain size due to fracturing, grinding and cracking by frictional heat. At greater depths, temperature increases and water under pressure becomes available. Water has the effect of weakening quartz grains so that they are made more plastic and they deform by becoming elongate and ribbon-shaped, rather than fracturing. Sheet silicates (micas, etc.) grow along quartz grain boundaries in shear zones, so that the resulting mylonites have a strongly developed directional fabric, which gives rise to cleavage planes. Chemical analyses of rocks in these shear zones have shown that they contain twice as much water as the surrounding rocks. Water may actually have moved along these shear zones during their formation, i.e. the shear zones acted as channelways for water transport during thrusting, thereby causing the rocks to be hydrated. High water pressures in fault zones have the added effect of lowering the resistance to friction between grains, i.e. water can weaken a fault zone and lubricate it, allowing sliding to take place more easily.

One of the best known thrusts in the world is the Moine Thrust Zone in north-west Scotland (Figs 3.6 & 13). The Moine Thrust Zone is a major tectonic structure, originating in the Caledonian orogeny, which contains metamorphic rocks and structures indicating that the thrust was an active zone for a long period of time. The thrust zone extends NE–SW and crops out continuously for 200 km from the north-west coast of Scotland to the south of the Isle of Skye in the Inner Hebrides (Fig. 3.6). It separates highly deformed and metamorphosed **Moine schists** (p. 75) on the east (i.e. above the thrust) from undeformed **Precambrian basement** (p. 2) rocks on the west, thereby forming the northwestern margin of the Caledonian orogenic belt in Scotland. A series of nappe folds (p. 33 & p. 71) occurs in the Moine rocks, individual nappes being separated from one another by eastwardly dipping thrust faults. During the orogeny, Moine rocks were folded into nappes which were transported northwestwards along these thrust planes over the underlying basement. The Moine Thrust Zone has a complex history of folding, faulting and metamorphism, which began with the formation of mylonites. Generally the mylonites are 100 m thick, but there are localities along the thrust zone where they attain thicknesses of 300 m or even 600–800 m.

Mylonites, like other metamorphic rocks, are derived from

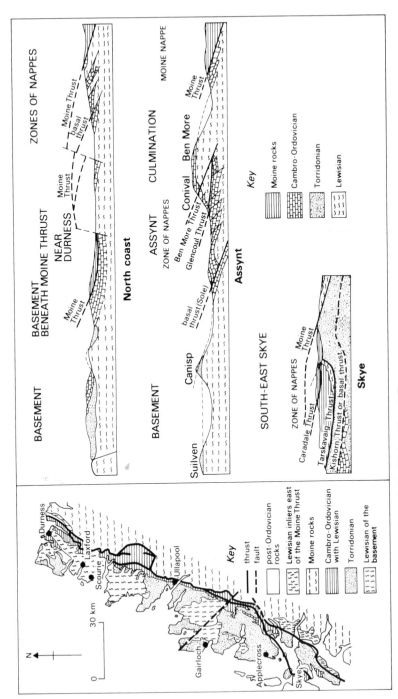

Figure 3.13 Map and sections through the Moine Thrust Zone.

pre-existing formations. In the case of the Moine Thrust mylonites, the rocks affected by thrusting were Cambro-Ordovician quartzites and shales and Lewisian gneiss. The resulting mylonites have the following mineral assemblages:

quartz mylonite: (from quartzite)	quartz–feldspar–mica
chlorite mylonite: (from shale)	chlorite–mica–quartz
'Lewisian' mylonite: (from hornblende– feldspar gneiss)	feldspar–epidote–chlorite

Mylonite belts have resulted from shearing of rocks during large-scale translation movements of the nappe folds along thrust planes. The mylonites are generally fine- to very fine-grained rocks with a banded structure; the grain size increases somewhat upwards through the mylonite zones. They have oriented fabrics and augen (p. 9) and 'ribbon' (p. 80) textures.

Detailed studies of grains in the quartz mylonites have been facilitated by the use of the electron microscope which can distinguish individual grains in the very fine-grained rocks where an ordinary microscope would not reveal much detail. Observations on these rocks show that there is a preferred alignment of quartz grain boundaries to form planar discontinuities, i.e. cleavage planes, in the mylonites. The quartz grain boundaries contain sheet silicates and tiny empty spaces (voids) which tend to weaken the quartz and allow deformation to take place more easily by grain boundary sliding, thereby elongating the quartz grains. This indicates that the cleavage planes in the mylonites are probably parallel to the shearing planes.

Beneath the mylonites is a series of thrust faults containing breccia, crushed rock and small amounts of pseudotachylyte formed by brittle deformation. These brittle thrusts cut the mylonites and are therefore younger. The overall history of the Moine Thrust Zone is that the mylonites formed by ductile deformation in shear zones at some considerable depth in the crust, associated with nappe folds; the zone was later uplifted to higher crustal levels, and movement accompanied by brittle deformation took place along a series of thrust faults. Figure 3.13 is a cross section through part of the Moine Thrust Zone, showing some of the complexity. It should be emphasised that the Moine Thrust proper is

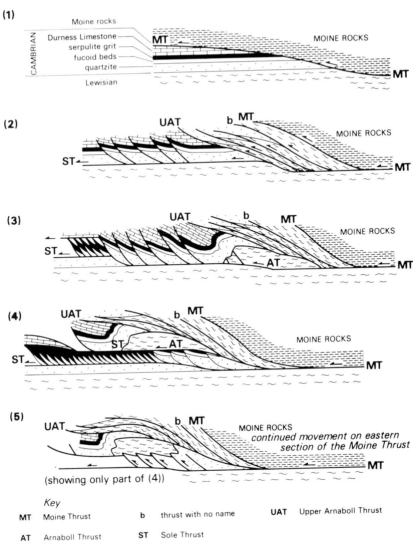

Figure 3.14 Possible evolutionary history of the Moine Thrust Zone on the north coast of Scotland. (1) Initial development of the Moine Thrust (MT), bringing Moine rocks from the east over the Cambro-Ordovician sequence; (2) large number of small thrusts result in slicing up of Lewisian Gneiss and Cambrian succession; (3) development of Arnaboll Nappe by generation of the Arnaboll Thrust (AT); at the front of the thrust belt, the Sole Thrust (ST) penetrates the Fucoid Beds and creates a zone of sliced rocks; (4) Arnaboll Thrust climbs up through the section and cuts through already sliced up rocks; (5) continued movement on the eastern portion of the Moine Thrust causes movement on the Sole Thrust and reactivation of minor faults and thrusts in the zone of sliced rocks. Note that in these sections the vertical scale is highly exaggerated; sections (1) to (5) are arranged in time sequence.

only one of a large set of thrust faults within a wide zone of nappes and thrusts, in which the nappes were stacked one on top of the other. Figure 3.14 shows possible stages in the evolution of the Moine Thrust Zone on the north coast of Scotland.

The Moine Thrust Zone is one of a series of Caledonian thrusts and together with the Outer Isles Thrust Zone is one of the last and most westerly to have developed. It has recently been suggested that the thrusts formed from a gently inclined shear zone at depth, with mylonites forming by intense ductile deformation. Nappes were piled one above the other as the edge of the orogenic belt was pushed out westwards over its basement.

Summary

Chapter 3 presented examples of different types of metamorphism: contact metamorphism in aureoles around large igneous intrusions and dynamic metamorphism in thrust fault zones.

Contact aureoles frequently contain a set of concentric metamorphic mineral zones around the intrusion, with different minerals and textures in each zone which reflect increasing temperature towards the intrusion. Spotted rocks and hornfelses result respectively from the low- and high-temperature metamorphism of pelitic sediments. Increasing temperatures cause dehydration of wet sediments and decarbonation of limestones.

Fault and thrust zones are characterised by high shearing stresses and high fluid partial pressures. Metamorphic rock types are breccia (fault crush rock), mylonites (banded, flinty rocks) and pseudotachylyte (intrusive glass). Water plays an important role in fault movements and metamorphism in fault zones, by lowering frictional resistance, by assisting grain boundary sliding, and by weakening quartz grains.

Exercises

1 The accompanying sketch map (Fig. 3.15) shows an area of sediments intruded by a large pluton of granodiorite. For each of the three localities A, B and C, describe the rock types and minerals you would be likely to find in the field. Mark on the map possible localities X, Y and Z where you might find rocks with the following mineral assemblages:

    X calcite + dolomite
    Y biotite + quartz + chiastolite
    Z sillimanite + quartz + biotite

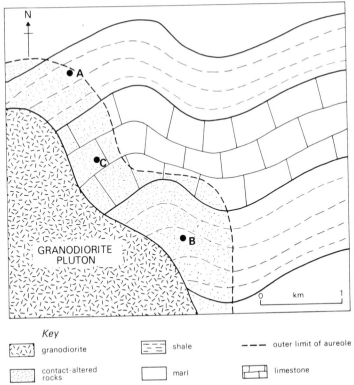

Figure 3.15 Sketch map of a granodioritic pluton that has intruded sedimentary rocks, showing a contact aureole.

2 Sketch a block diagram of an area which has a near-vertical granitic pluton intruding sediments. Insert and label the following features on your diagram:

(a) unaltered sedimentary rocks;
(b) low, medium and high-grade contact metamorphic zones.

3 List the index minerals in metamorphosed pelitic sediments and group them according to metamorphic grade.

4 Metamorphic terrains II

Regional metamorphism

Most metamorphic rocks occur in **fold mountain chains** or in continental **shields**, which may be the eroded root zones of ancient mountain chains. Such metamorphic rocks therefore cover large areas of the continental crust (Fig. 4.1). They are termed regional metamorphic rocks and they include such types as **schists** and gneisses. Regional metamorphic rocks arise by the combined action of heat, burial pressure, differential stress, strain and fluids on pre-existing rocks (see p. 3 & pp. 20–25 for an explanation of these terms). The resulting rocks are always deformed and they exhibit such characteristics as folds and cleavages (Fig. 4.2). Large amounts of granite are often associated with regional metamorphic rocks, for reasons that will be explained later (p. 88).

As in contact metamorphic rocks, certain index minerals grow in response to increasing pressure and temperature. These index minerals are used in the field to define regional zones of increasing metamorphic grade.

Regional metamorphism covers a wide range of pressure and temperature conditions, roughly from 200 °C to 750 °C and 2 kbar to 10 kbar (5–35 km depth, approximately). It is necessary to divide this wide range up into smaller, more manageable segments that reflect geological environments. The means used to subdivide the pressure–temperature space of regional metamorphism into different fields is the mineral assemblage of metamorphic rocks. The results of laboratory experiments on the growth and stability of metamorphic minerals at various pressures and temperatures are incorporated with microscope studies of the mineral assemblages, textures and fabrics of metamorphic rocks to provide estimates of the conditions of metamorphism. Rock types that respond most readily to variations in pressure and temperature are fine-grained pelitic sediments (shales and mudstones) and basic igneous rocks with the composition of basaltic lavas. These are the types that are used to define regional metamorphic **facies** (p. 40) in orogenic belts.

Regional metamorphism of pelitic rocks. The study of metamorphic rocks was begun in a serious way about a century ago by geologists such as George Barrow who worked in the **Dalradian schists** of the

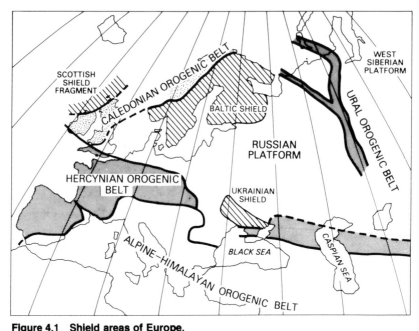

Figure 4.1   Shield areas of Europe.

south-west Scottish Highlands (Fig. 3.6). There, the metamorphosed
pelitic and basic rocks contain a large number of silicate minerals, and
Barrow made the observation that some of these minerals could be used
as indicators of metamorphic grade. Table 4.1 lists the common silicates
found in metamorphosed pelitic and basic rocks. Minerals used as
metamorphic indicators are marked with an asterisk in the table. The
minerals which are likely to be unfamiliar to you are andalusite, kyanite,
sillimanite, cordierite and staurolite (see Table 1.1). Note especially that
the minerals in Table 4.1 cannot all be found together in the same rock.
Andalusite, kyanite and sillimanite are described as the aluminosilicate
polymorphs (p. 11): although they have the same composition, the three
varieties have quite different crystal structures and physical properties
(see Fig. 4.3 & Table 1.1). They are sensitive to pressure and temperature changes and usually only one of the polymorphs is present in a
particular metamorphosed pelitic rock of the appropriate composition.

Figure 4.2   Photographs of deformed rocks. (a) Folds in banded gneiss, Karelia,
USSR; (b) steep schist belt cutting through banded granulite, Lewisian Gneiss Complex;
(c) schist in shear belt cutting through coarse hornblende–feldspar gneiss, Lewisian
Gneiss Complex.

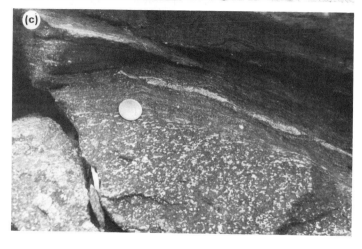

Table 4.1 Regional metamorphic zones and mineral assemblages in different original rock types (* index mineral).

Grade (rock name)	Mineral zone (for pelitic rocks)	Mineral assemblage produced		
		mudstones and shales	limestones	basic igneous rocks
low (slate, phyllite) (schist)	chlorite	chlorite*, quartz, muscovite, plagioclase	chlorite*, calcite or dolomite, plagioclase	chlorite*, plagioclase
	biotite	biotite*, quartz, plagioclase		
medium (schist)	garnet	garnet*, mica, quartz, plagioclase	garnet*, epidote, hornblende, calcite	garnet*, chlorite epidote, plagioclase
	staurolite	staurolite*, mica, garnet, quartz, plagioclase		
high (gneiss)	kyanite	kyanite*, mica, garnet, quartz, plagioclase	garnet, hornblende*, plagioclase	hornblende*, plagioclase
	sillimanite	sillimanite*, garnet, mica, quartz, plagioclase	garnet, augite*, plagioclase	

These three minerals have been studied extensively in the laboratory and a good deal is known about their pressure and temperature controls and their stability under varying metamorphic conditions. When a critical temperature or pressure value is reached, one variety **transforms** to another, i.e.:

andalusite $\rightleftharpoons$ kyanite   (pressure increase)
andalusite $\rightleftharpoons$ sillimanite (temperature increase)
kyanite $\rightleftharpoons$ sillimanite   (temperature increase)

Double arrows here mean that the transformations are reversible, i.e. they can go in either direction. Figure 4.4 is a pressure–temperature graph showing the fields in which each of the Al_2SiO_5 polymorphs is stable. One polymorph transforms to another across the lines on the graph. Figure 4.4 has been constructed from data obtained in the laboratory under controlled conditions. The triple point (where the three lines meet on the graph) is the pressure–temperature value at which all three polymorphs can theoretically exist in equilibrium. Laboratory investigations of the aluminosilicates have produced at least 13 different determinations for the triple point, due to differences in methods, equipment and techniques. The consensus view is that the triple point is located at approximately 4 kb ($\equiv 14$ km depth) and 500 °C. Notice on Figure 4.4 that, since hyanite occupies an area along the pressure axis, it must be the pressure-sensitive form. Similarly, sillimanite occurs to the right of the diagram, and is therefore the temperature-sensitive polymorph (temperature increases to the right on Fig. 4.4).

In order to illustrate particular aspects of the regional metamorphism of sediments and lavas, the Dalradian rocks of Scotland will be used as an example.

In the Scottish Highlands the Dalradian rocks crop out over a wide area north of the Highland Boundary Fault and south of the Great Glen Fault, and in the Shetland Islands (Figs 3.6 & 4.5). They are a group of sediments and lavas, deformed and metamorphosed during the Caledonian orogeny, which reached its maximum intensity around 500 Ma ago and ended about 400 Ma ago. Fragments of the Caledonian mountain chain are exposed in the Appalachians and in Scandinavia, as well as in Scotland (Fig. 4.6). The mountain chain would be continuous if the eastern seaboard of North America were attached to western Europe. By implication, the two continents were once united in a larger land mass, at least during the period of the Caledonian orogeny, which later split up and the separate continents drifted apart (Fig. 4.6; see p. 75).

(a)

(b)

Figure 4.3   Hand specimens of Al$_2$SiO$_5$ polymorphs. (a) andalusite; (b) kyanite; (c) sillimanite (small white nodules).

Some theories concerning the possible causes of the Caledonian orogeny will be discussed later, after we have investigated the metamorphic processes which affected Dalradian rocks during the orogeny.

The Dalradian rocks are a very mixed succession, amounting to a

(c)

Figure 4.3 – *continued*.

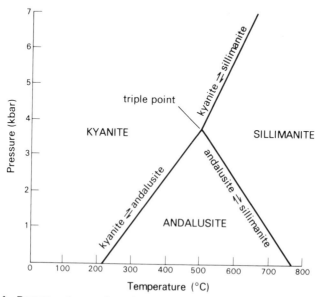

Figure 4.4 Pressure–temperature dependence of the three Al₂SIO₅ polymorphs.

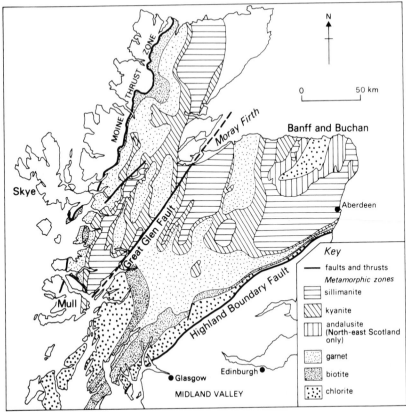

Figure 4.5 The Dalradian and Moine rocks in the Scottish Highlands, showing Barrow's and Buchan metamorphic zones for pelitic rocks.

stratigraphic thickness totalling some 13 km of conglomerates, sand-stones, siltstones, mudstones, shales, limestones, lavas and tuffs. The stratigraphy of these rocks is shown in simplified form in Figure 4.7. Although the rocks are now metamorphosed, their original structures and compositions are still recognisable in many instances. The rocks were deposited during late Precambrian and Cambrian times in a deep sedimentary basin. During the Caledonian orogeny, they were deformed into a series of major nappe folds, as a result of which rocks are upside down in some places (Fig. 4.8). Dalradian rocks are cut by many large granites (Fig. 4.9), which were intruded towards the end of the Caledonian orogeny and after the main regional metamorphism of the Dalradian rocks. Some of these granites have contact metamorphic aureoles around them.

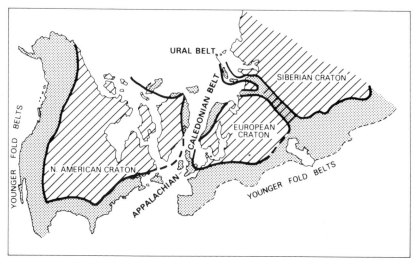

Figure 4.6 Caledonian–Appalachian orogenic belt. A reconstruction before continental drifting and the opening of the modern Atlantic Ocean.

The Dalradian rocks of the south-west Highlands were subdivided by Barrow into a set of metamorphic zones, commonly referred to as **Barrow's zones** which indicate the first appearance of an index mineral in metamorphosed pelitic sediments. The sequence of zones, indicating increasing metamorphic grade is: chlorite → biotite → garnet → staurolite → kyanite → sillimanite. Some of the minerals that crystallise at low grades are stable at higher grades, e.g. garnet schists may contain biotite as well as garnet. Figure 4.5 shows the outcrop of the metamorphic zones in Dalradian and other rocks of the Caledonian orogeny. Notice from the map (Fig. 4.5) that a separate, distinct set of zones exists for the Dalradian rocks in the north-east of Scotland. There the zones are referred to as the **Buchan zones** after the Banff and Buchan District of Scotland, where they occur. The Buchan zones have the following sequence of index minerals: chlorite → biotite → cordierite → andalusite → sillimanite. As in Barrow's zones, metamorphic grade increases from left to right in this sequence. The Buchan mineral zones are also for metamorphosed pelitic sediments. The difference in the two sequences reflects different metamorphic conditions in the two areas, primarily differences in geothermal gradients (p. 22), as well as certain differences in original rock composition. This will be discussed in greater detail later (p. 82).

Taking shales as the starting point, the first changes in response to

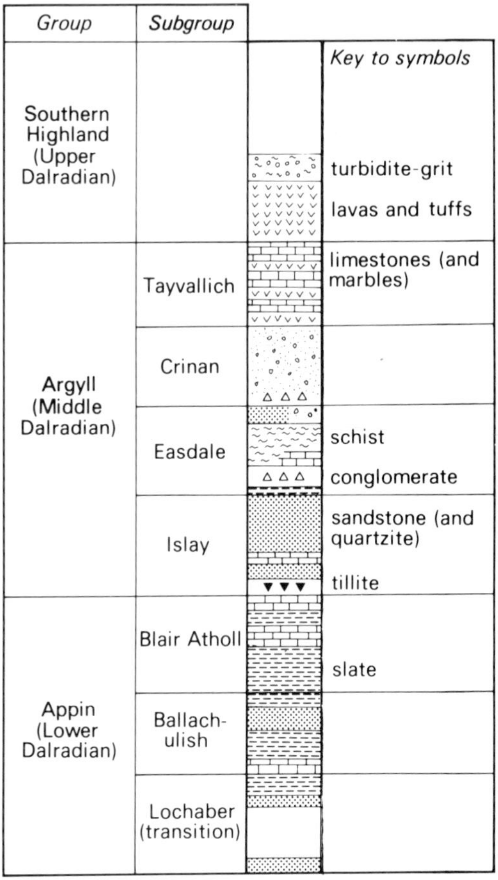

Group	Subgroup		
			Key to symbols
Southern Highland (Upper Dalradian)			turbidite-grit
			lavas and tuffs
Argyll (Middle Dalradian)	Tayvallich		limestones (and marbles)
	Crinan		
	Easdale		schist
			conglomerate
	Islay		sandstone (and quartzite)
			tillite
Appin (Lower Dalradian)	Blair Atholl		slate
	Ballach-ulish		
	Lochaber (transition)		

Figure 4.7   Stratigraphic subdivision of Dalradian rocks in Scotland.

increasing pressure and temperature result in the formation of a slate. Clay minerals become recrystallised to give chlorite and muscovite. These micas tend to lie parallel to each other and at right angles to the maximum stress direction (p. 25). As a consequence, slates develop a slaty cleavage. Slaty cleavage is not always related to bedding and may cut across it (Fig. 4.10). Slates are fissile and will usually break cleanly (or **cleave**) along cleavage planes.

With increasing temperature, the rock becomes coarser grained owing to crystal growth and it is more or less completely recrystallised. The resulting rock type is a **phyllite.** Phyllites are rich in platy minerals, particularly chlorite, which gives them a pale green colour and lustrous

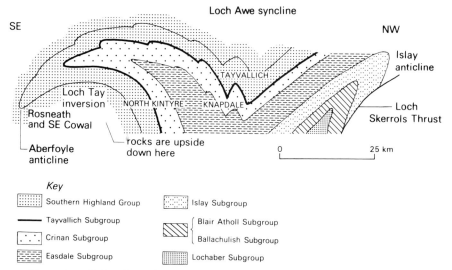

Figure 4.8 **Folded Dalradian rocks in the south-west Highlands of Scotland.** Rocks in some places are overturned.

sheen, due to tiny reflecting cleavage surfaces which are lined up. Phyllites are strongly cleaved rocks, but the cleavage is often crinkled or rumpled like little waves, with the crests of the waves lined up, defining a lineation (Fig. 4.11). Phyllites form when the temperature is in the approximate range 300–350 °C.

A further increase in temperature (and metamorphic grade) causes biotite to grow if potassium is present, at the expense mainly of chlorite and muscovite. Grain size increases by continued grain growth, and the typical rock produced is a schist. Depending on which mica predominates, the rock may be called a biotite schist, a muscovite schist or simply a mica schist.

Eventually a fundamental change occurs in the progressive metamorphism of pelitic sediments with the separation or **segregation** of quartz into independent, little, narrow streaks, zones, ribbons or layers. Quartz segregation results from **pressure solution**, which is a process that takes place during deformation under metamorphic conditions of sediments. Pressure solution also operates during the diagenesis of quartz-rich sediments, particularly sandstones, and results in quartz grains being welded together (Fig. 4.12). In pressure solution, material is selectively dissolved away at particular points on the surface of a mineral (often quartz) and the dissolved material is removed by circulating fluids to be deposited elsewhere. The actual amount of movement

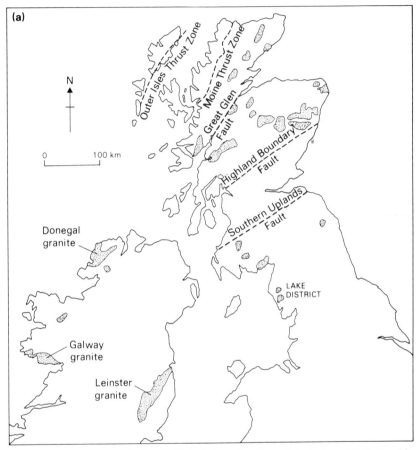

Figure 4.9 **(a)** **Map of the British Isles showing Caledonian granites.** **(b)** **Distribution of regional migmatites in the Caledonian belt of the Scottish Highlands.** Younger (post-tectonic) granites are numbered: 1, Lairg; 2, Migdale; 3, Strontian; 4, Peterhead; 5, Foyers; 6, Moy; 7, Monadhliath; 8, Cairngorm; 9, Lochnagar; 10, Hill of Fare; 11, Battock; 12, Rannoch; 13, Etive; 14, Glen Fyne.

may be quite restricted and, in the case of schists, the quartz within segregations probably has been transported in solution only a few millimetres, i.e. it is 'local' and has not been introduced into the schist from outside. This means that the overall (or bulk) chemical composition of a schist will be quite close to that of the sediment from which it was derived. Schists may often have a banded appearance, light-coloured quartz being interbanded with dark mica. This banding has nothing to

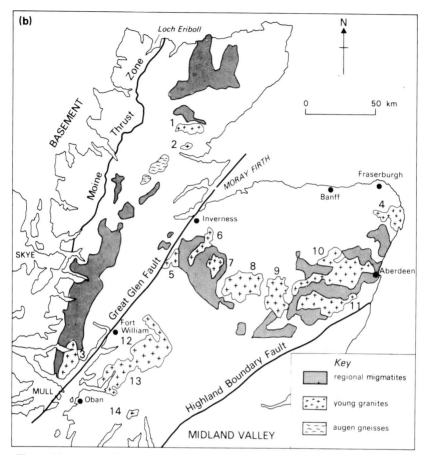

Figure 4.9 – *continued*

do with bedding. At temperatures of around 400–450 °C the new mineral garnet makes its first appearance, although biotite is still stable in the **garnet zone**. A typical rock is garnet–mica schist. Garnets can grow quite large (Fig. 4.13), forming euhedral porphyroblasts with well formed crystal faces. In a garnet–mica schist the planar structure is less pronounced than in a slate. Banding is uneven and the rock takes on a foliated texture, in which there are bands or layers of different minerals, with micas showing strong preferred orientation. Schists and rocks of higher metamorphic grade do not usually preserve bedding or other original features.

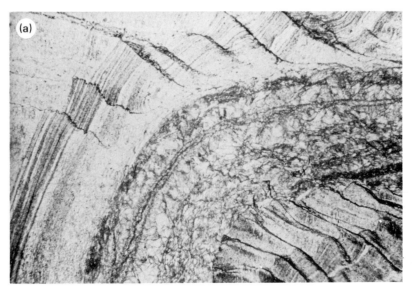

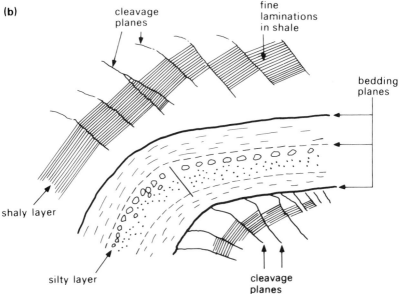

Figure 4.10 Folded silty and shaly sediment. Photograph of thin section to show relation between bedding and slaty cleavage; cleavage planes form in shale but not in silt layers.

Figure 4.11 Hand specimen of phyllite, deformed by small folds.

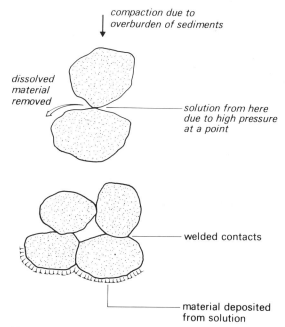

compaction due to
overburden of sediments

dissolved
material
removed

solution from here
due to high pressure
at a point

welded contacts

material deposited
from solution

Figure 4.12 How grains are welded together by pressure solution.

Figure 4.13   Eye-shaped porphyroblast of garnet (dark and round) with mica in the corners of the eye, in a matrix of quartz (white and grey) and mica (small, distinct needles). Photograph of a thin section of quartz–garnet–mica schist.

A typical mineral assemblage in pelitic sediments of the garnet zone is:

quartz + muscovite + biotite + garnet + plagioclase

and for metamorphosed basic igneous rocks:

hornblende + plagioclase + garnet + biotite

It has been mentioned previously that the Dalradian rocks contain limestones (Fig. 4.7). These have produced marbles with the following typical mineral assemblages in the garnet zone:

calcite + pyroxene + garnet

and:

calcite + hornblende

In the case of these metamorphosed carbonate rocks, the pyroxene and garnet are calcium-rich varieties, while in pelitic sediments the garnet is iron-rich.

Foliated and banded rocks are important at higher metamorphic grades. The tendency for minerals to segregate into alternating bands of different minerals becomes more pronounced at high grades. Grain size also increases and minerals in individual bands are closely interlocked. The result is a coarse, banded rock called gneiss. Gneiss has light-coloured bands of quartz and feldspar (white, pink or cream) and dark bands of biotite and hornblende (black). Although the rock is banded, it does not split easily into planar fragments unless there is a large amount of biotite. Kyanite and sillimanite are the index minerals used in these high-grade rocks. Gneisses of non-sedimentary origin are discussed on page 84. In schists and gneisses containing staurolite and kyanite, these minerals are frequently porphyroblastic (indeed, many of the Barrow's index minerals occur as porphyroblasts). Staurolite may form stumpy prismatic crystals, sometimes developing cross-shaped twins, whereas kyanite usually forms long, thin, flat bluish blades (Fig. 4.3). Sillimanite, on the other hand, often occurs as bundles of tiny fibres or needles, sometimes associated with biotite. It may be difficult to identify in a gneiss, although the illustration shown here (Fig. 4.3) is of small eye-shaped 'nodules' of quartz intergrown with sillimanite.

Typical mineral assemblages in the staurolite, kyanite and sillimanite zones in different rock compositions are set out in Table 4.1. Note from this table that the index minerals (staurolite, kyanite and sillimanite) occur only in pelitic sediments, i.e. they had a suitable original composition to allow these minerals to form. Carbonate sediments and basic igneous rocks have different (and 'less sensitive') compositions, so they show only two zones or one zone respectively, compared to the three zones in pelitic rocks.

Because Barrow's zones were established early in the history of the study of metamorphic rocks, they were accepted as the norm for a long time. The sequences of metamorphic zones in other parts of the world, such as Norway, the Appalachians in north-east United States and New Zealand when mapped turned out to be similar (but not identical) to Barrow's zones in the Scottish Dalradian rocks. However, it was soon discovered that completely different sequences were possible. Only 60 km to the north of Barrow's type area, on the Banff and Buchan coast (Fig. 4.5) the Dalradian rocks were shown to contain a different sequence of mineral assemblages. The two types of metamorphic sequence are characterised by the Al_2SiO_5 polymorphs they contain, i.e.

(a) Barrow type: develops first kyanite, then sillimanite with increasing metamorphic grade in pelitic rocks;
(b) Buchan type: develops first andalusite, then sillimanite with increasing grade in pelitic rocks.

These two sequences indicate that local differences in metamorphism and crustal conditions are possible within the same orogenic belt. The Barrow-type sequence is medium- to high-pressure, medium-temperature metamorphism (kyanite → sillimanite), and the Buchan-type sequence is high-temperature–low-pressure metamorphism (andalusite → sillimanite). It has been estimated that at the peak of metamorphism, the rocks in Barrow's sillimanite zone were at a depth of about 12 km. In north-east Scotland on the other hand, the Dalradian rocks may only have been buried to a depth of 3 or 4 km. To obtain the Buchan-type metamorphic sequence there must have been high heat flow and a steep geothermal gradient (i.e. high temperatures at shallow depths in the crust, see p. 23). In north-east Scotland there is a strong relationship between the Dalradian rocks and plutonic igneous rocks, notably granites and gabbros, as shown in Figure 4.9b. It is possible that in the area of Buchan-type metamorphism additional heat was brought into the orogenic belt by convection. A significant fact concerning the Buchan area is the presence of rocks that seem to have formed by partial melting (discussed in greater detail on p. 88), requiring an influx of heat. These particular rocks are associated with the sillimanite (high-temperature) zone.

Metamorphic rocks in Precambrian shields

The cores of all the continents in the world are occupied by the great shields which account for considerable areas and volumes of the continental crust (Fig. 4.1). Shields consist mainly of metamorphic rocks of Precambrian age unconformably overlain by younger non-metamorphic sediments. Surrounding these Precambrian continental cores are younger fold mountain belts. Shield areas contain the remnants (often as separated fragments) of Precambrian orogenic belts which over millions of years of erosion have been elevated to their present levels, thereby allowing us to see deep inside these ancient orogenic belts. By and large, shield areas have relatively gentle, low-lying topography. The presence of remnants of old mountain belts becomes evident only after mapping structural trends in the shields. Shield areas are stable blocks of thick continental crust which have low heat-flow values (p. 23), reflecting the fact that orogenic activity ceased a long time ago. They are also often referred to as **cratons** or **platforms**. The age structure of continental shields is such that the oldest orogenic fragments are at the centres of shields and are surrounded by younger Precambrian orogenic belts (e.g. Fig. 4.14 is a map showing the age pattern of rocks in North America, with the oldest parts of the Canadian Shield at the very centre).

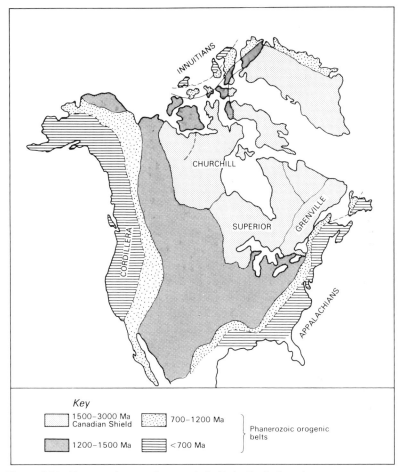

Figure 4.14 Pattern of ages of orogenic belts in North America.

In general terms, the most common metamorphic rocks of Precambrian shields are banded gneisses of granitic composition, but relatively narrow belts of sediments and lavas, often showing low metamorphic grades, play an important, if subsidiary, role in the structure of most shields. The significance of the structure of shields is discussed later (Ch. 5). In addition to gneisses, there are frequent but small patches of the very high-grade metamorphic rock known as **granulite** (p. 86), a rock devoid of hydrous minerals which formed at high temperatures (800–900 °C approximately). Granulites mostly occur in the oldest parts of shields, but there are a few occurrences around the world of granulites in younger fold mountain belts.

The rocks of the Lewisian Gneiss Complex in the north-west Highlands of Scotland (Fig. 3.6) will be used as an example to illustrate the structure and composition of Precambrian shields. On a global scale, the gneisses of north-west Scotland are only a tiny fragment of a shield, but they do nevertheless contain most of the rock types found in much larger shields. Before the relatively recent opening of the Atlantic Ocean, the Lewisian Gneiss Complex formed part of the shield area of a great northern continent (or 'supercontinent') that stretched from Canada across Greenland to Scotland and Scandinavia. There are many similarities in the rock types, ages and structures of the Canadian, Greenland, Scottish and Baltic Shields which indicate that they once formed a single crustal block (or continental plate).

In north-west Scotland the oldest rocks are granulites and gneisses, which have been dated at 2900 Ma old (this is the age of the peak of the main metamorphism recorded in these rocks). These old rocks occupy a central portion of the Scottish shield fragment and are surrounded by granitic gneisses, granites and pegmatites, which have predominant ages of 1800 Ma. In the Lewisian Gneiss Complex there were at least two major **orogenic events**, separated by several hundreds of millions of years. An orogenic event is part of a cycle involving the deposition of sediments and the eruption of lavas, their folding, metamorphism and intrusion by igneous rocks, followed by the uplift, erosion and stabilisation of the crustal segment that was subjected to the orogeny.

Typical rocks in the central block of the Lewisian Complex are granulites and gneisses, varying in composition from ultrabasic to intermediate. This variation reflects the original compositions of the rocks, many of which were igneous. In granulite, the anhydrous minerals feldspar, pyroxene, garnet and quartz occur. These minerals are approximately equidimensional in external shape, in contrast to flat micas and elongate amphiboles (note also that micas and amphiboles are hydrous minerals). Granulites generally have granoblastic textures (p. 8) in which all the minerals are of approximately the same size and shape. Although a mineral banding may be present (e.g. pyroxene bands alternating with feldspar bands), granulites by and large are devoid of directional fabrics. Common mineral assemblages of the granulites and gneisses are:

quartz + plagioclase + pyroxene + iron ore
plagioclase + pyroxene + iron ore
pyroxene + garnet + iron ore
plagioclase + pyroxene + garnet + iron ore
pyroxene + olivine + iron ore

Iron-magnesium silicates predominate in these assemblages and it is possible that many of the metamorphic rocks have been derived from plutonic igneous rocks. Some of the basic and ultrabasic gneisses have margins and internal structures, textures and fabrics indicating that they were intruded as sheets of magma into the orogenic belt. Laboratory studies of these assemblages have led geologists to conclude that the rocks were probably metamorphosed under very high pressure and temperature conditions, i.e. about 900 °C and 10 kbar ($\equiv$ 35–40 km depth).

The rocks of the Lewisian Complex show evidence of having been affected several times by metamorphism. In the case of pyroxene- and olivine-bearing gneisses, later metamorphic events were retrogressive (p. 11) and were marked by the introduction of water. Hydrous minerals (micas or amphiboles) partially or completely replaced the minerals formed during an earlier metamorphic episode. In particular, pyroxene is often rimmed by tiny crystals of hornblende (Fig. 4.15), and olivine is nearly always replaced by serpentine, i.e.:

$$\text{olivine} + \text{water} \xrightarrow{\ heat\ } \text{serpentine} + \text{magnetite}$$

Within the area occupied by granulites and pyroxene gneisses there are a few small remnants of pelitic rocks (referred to as **metasediments**)

Figure 4.15   Granulite. Photograph of a thin section in which tiny crystals of amphibole have grown along pyroxene grain boundaries to form a rim.

which have mineral assemblages similar in some respects to those in the higher of Barrow's metamorphic zones. The aluminosilicates are kyanite and sillimanite, and the presence of abundant micas tends to make the rocks schistose.

In the central block of the outcrop of the Lewisian Gneiss Complex, the gneisses and granulites are roughly compositionally banded on the scale of about one metre, with the banding being near horizontal or gently inclined. This is in contrast to the gneisses north and south of the central block which have a pronounced banding that dips steeply owing to folding. Additionally, the composition of the rocks is different, with pyroxene gneiss and granulite absent and quartz–feldspar–biotite–hornblende gneiss predominating. Veins and sheets of granite and pegmatite are common in the northern and southern blocks as intrusive igneous bodies. Typical mineral assemblages of the gneisses are:

feldspar + quartz + hornblende + biotite

and

hornblende + feldspar + garnet

Potassium is an important element (which is absent from the granulites and pyroxene gneisses) occurring in potash feldspar and biotite. Hydrous minerals are common in the gneisses, indicating that water was present during metamorphism. The overall composition of the quartz–feldspar gneisses is broadly granodioritic and granitic, and it is possible that the rocks were initially intermediate to acidic lavas and tuffs with minor amounts of sediments, intruded by acidic igneous bodies. Hornblende–feldspar gneiss could have formed from a basaltic lava or a dolerite sill. Banding in gneisses is on the scale of a hand specimen, quartz–feldspar bands alternating with hornblende–biotite bands, to give a characteristic black and white striped appearance. Directional fabrics are common, and banded gneisses frequently have foliated and lineated textures (Fig. 4.16).

The origin of gneissose banding is a matter of some debate and a number of different theories exist. It would probably be true to say that there is banding and banding, i.e. banding in gneisses is of several different types and could have formed in a variety of ways. In the case of the ultrabasic gneisses in the central block, the bands are of different mineral compositions (pyroxenes alternating with olivine) that could have been inherited from when the rocks were intruded as magma, with different mineral bands settling out under gravity. As far as the metasediments are concerned, banding is parallel to compositional layering and

Figure 4.16 Photographs of gneisses and migmatites. (a) Banded gneiss cut by pegmatite sheet, Lewisian Complex; (b) banded gneiss showing boudin structure and development of granitic material in neck of boudin, Helsinki, Finland; (c) folded, deformed basic dykes (dark) cutting through very coarse, strongly banded gneiss, Karelia, USSR; (d) folds in coarse migmatitic gneiss, Helsinki, Finland; (e) patchy migmatite with blocks of dark hornblende gneiss surrounded by pale granitic material, Karelia, Finland; (f) folds in calc-silicate rock (impure marble).

Figure 4.16 – *continued.*

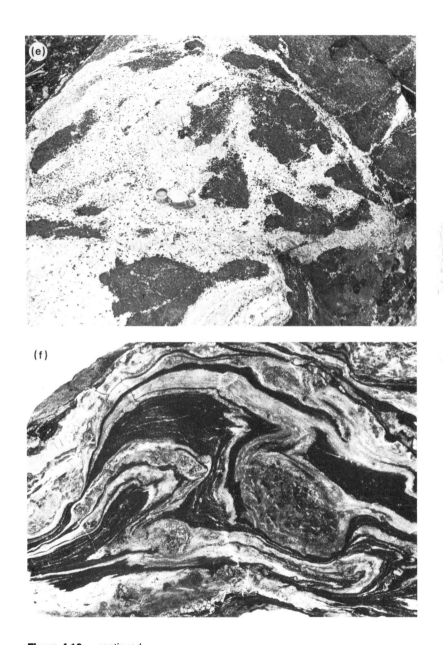

Figure 4.16 – *continued.*

it could reflect original sedimentary differences (this is *not* the same as saying that gneissose banding equals bedding). In intermediate granulites the banding is such that broad compositional changes in bands are about a metre apart, which might reflect original differences in the composition of lavas and tuffs. Deformation has usually been so intense that the metamorphic rocks have been extensively flattened. As far as the quartz–feldspar gneisses are concerned, some of the banding could have been produced during metamorphism by the migration of certain components. Potassium, sodium, silicon and a few other elements are relatively mobile and could have migrated during metamorphism into layers and formed feldspar and quartz. The migration of these components would have left behind iron and magnesium, which then formed ferromagnesian minerals (hornblende and biotite) in separate layers. The scale of this migration could have been local (a few millimetres or centimetres) to give banded gneisses in which bands are 1–2 cm thick.

Throughout the northern and southern blocks of the Lewisian Complex **migmatite** is a common rock. Migmatite is (literally) a 'mixed rock' in which granitic material in the form of veins, streaks and lenses has invaded or been intermixed with high-grade metamorphic rocks of a different composition. In the case of migmatites among the Lewisian gneisses, the high-grade metamorphic rock is often hornblende–feldspar gneiss (Fig. 4.16), but pelitic rocks are also mixed with granitic material to form migmatite. If banding is present in migmatites, it is usually irregular and can best be observed in the field at outcrop scale. Migmatites contain the same minerals as the gneisses with which they are associated, i.e. feldspar, quartz, hornblende, biotite and garnet. The presence of the hydrous minerals hornblende and biotite may reflect invasion by a water-rich melt from a deeper, now dry, environment. It has been proposed that the quartz–feldspar gneisses in the Lewisian Complex formed above granulites and pyroxene gneisses, which formed at 35–40 km depth. During the formation of granulites, water was completely expelled and could have migrated upwards, carrying potassium and certain other elements. This flux of water would then have played an important role in the formation of quartz–feldspar gneisses and migmatites at higher levels in the crust.

Migmatites are thought to have formed by partial melting during metamorphism. Partial melting is possible in high-grade metamorphism provided that water is present and the rocks have a suitable composition. In the presence of water, quartz and feldspar can melt together at around 750 °C to give a liquid of granitic composition, leaving the remaining part of the rock unmolten. This granitic material is generally less dense than the surrounding solid rocks and tends to rise and invade other rocks at higher levels. The granitic material may eventually merge together to form a body of magma at higher levels in the crust, producing a granite pluton. At lower levels, where partial melting takes place, the granitic material may migrate to invade metamorphic rocks and form migmatites. Migration distances need not be large, for the granitic component of many migmatites is thought to be quite local, of the order of centimetres or metres. This means that, on the scale of metres, metamorphism has not involved any substantial addition or removal of material (other than water and a few mobile elements).

Of common occurrence in the central block of the Lewisian Gneiss outcrop are steep or vertical, narrow (1–10 m, up to 100 m wide), long (at least 1–2 km) shear belts consisting of finely banded gneisses and schists with pronounced directional fabrics, i.e. micas forming a schistosity and hornblendes a lineation. Hydrous minerals, micas and amphiboles, occur together with quartz, feldspar and garnet. The rocks of the shear belts were formed by the **retrogressive** metamorphism of the granulites and pyroxene gneisses which they cut. A combination of heat, high strain and water caused chemical reactions that led to the formation of amphibole from pyroxene and mica from amphibole. Within the shear belts, retrogressive metamorphism was usually so complete that all traces of the pyroxene gneiss mineral assemblages have been obliterated. Detailed chemical studies of mineral assemblages and individual mineral grains have allowed the conclusion to be drawn that the shear belts acted as channelways for hydrous fluids, which were expelled from granulites at depth and migrated upwards. Shear belts acted as movement zones within which deformation was intense and water vapour pressure was high. It has been suggested that shear belts, which are found in all Precambrian shields, often as parallel sets, are the deep crustal equivalents of faults in brittle rocks at higher crustal levels which once overlay the metamorphic rocks of the lower crust. It can sometimes be shown by mapping across shear belts that there has been displacement of the rocks on either side. (See the section on dynamic metamorphism dealing with the possible origin of the Moine Thrust Zone, p. 61.)

High-pressure–low-temperature regional metamorphism

In certain parts of the world geologically young orogenic belts, mainly of Cenozoic and Mesozoic age, contain areas of metamorphosed greywackes and basic volcanic rocks with unusual blue amphiboles. The rocks are often (but not always) schistose and they may have a characteristic blue colour, hence they are called **blueschists**. As well as amphibole, the blueschists may contain pyroxene, sheet silicates and feldspar-like hydrated silicates with compositions that indicate metamorphism under conditions of unusually low heat flow, low temperature and high pressure. Original features may be preserved in cases where deformation has not been intense, such as graded bedding in greywackes or pillow structure in lavas, due to the fact that the low temperatures of metamorphism were insufficient to cause complete recrystallisation.

Most blueschist occurrences are in the circum-Pacific zone or the Alpine–Himalayan chain (Fig. 2.10), but there are occasional remnants in Palaeozoic orogenic belts, e.g. in Anglesey, Wales, in the Caledonian belt. Blueschists are absent from Precambrian orogenic belts, for reasons dealt with later (p. 113). In terms of global tectonics blueschists occur in orogenic belts at continent/continent and continent/ocean plate collision zones (Fig. 2.11, Ch. 5).

An example of blueschist metamorphism occurs in the Franciscan area in the Coast Ranges of California, west of the Sierra Nevada (Fig. 4.17). The Franciscan rocks were deposited as a 15–20 km thick sequence of greywackes and basalts onto the ocean floor during late Jurassic and Cretaceous time. The rocks were regionally metamorphosed at least twice, about 150 Ma ago and again at 120–100 Ma ago, under low-temperature–high-pressure conditions. Recrystallisation was incomplete and patchy throughout the region due to the low-temperature nature of the metamorphism, so that the rocks tend to be non-schistose and to preserve original sedimentary structures and textures. Incomplete recrystallisation is also indicated by the lack of equilibrium between the relatively large number of different minerals (up to a dozen or so are possible) in the blueschists. Laboratory studies of the minerals in blueschists indicate metamorphism at around 300–400 °C and 8–10 kbar.

Blueschists in the Franciscan rocks occur adjacent to an ocean trench and above a subduction zone. Heat flow in such a tectonic environment is low because cold lithosphere is being dragged (or subducted) down into the higher-temperature mantle (Fig. 4.18). Heat is transferred by conduction and the descending slab of lithosphere does not have time to heat up to the same temperature as the surrounding mantle rocks. As the slab is dragged down to greater depths, pressure and strain increase with the result that the metamorphism is of the high-pressure, high-strain, low-temperature type. In this plate tectonic model of the Earth's behaviour, ocean crust (basaltic in composition) is dragged down into the upper mantle in subduction zones. At depths of 50 km or more, this

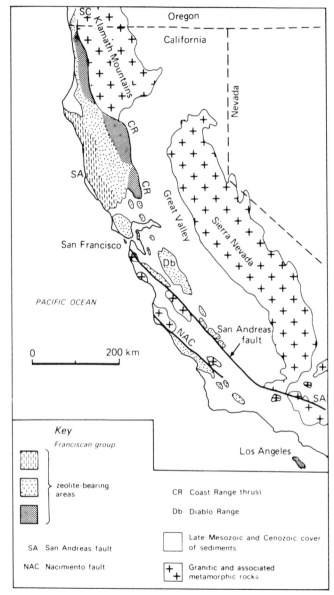

Oregon

California

Nevada

SC

Klamath Mountains

CR

SA

CR

Great Valley

Sierra Nevada

San Francisco

Db

PACIFIC OCEAN

NAC

San Andreas fault

0   200 km

SA

Los Angeles

Key

Franciscan group

zeolite-bearing areas

CR   Coast Range thrust

Db   Diablo Range

SA   San Andreas fault

NAC Nacimiento fault

Late Mesozoic and Cenozoic cover of sediments

Granitic and associated metamorphic rocks

Figure 4.17 Geological sketch map of California, showing metamorphic and instrusive rocks.

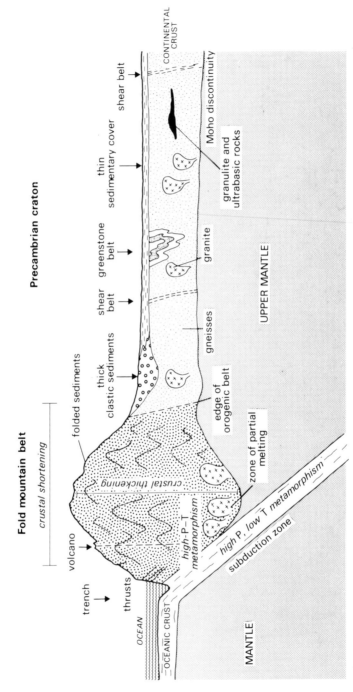

Figure 4.18 Cross section through a hypothetical subduction zone, showing locations of metamorphic rocks.

basalt is metamorphosed at very high pressures to a dense rock of the same bulk chemical composition known as **eclogite**, which has the mineral assemblage: pyroxene + garnet. Eclogite is a rare rock and is found infrequently in orogenic belts, sometimes associated with blueschists. It also occurs occasionally as xenoliths in basic volcanic rocks and is thought to have travelled up from the upper mantle.

It was mentioned previously that blueschists are largely restricted to young orogenic belts. This is not to say that the metamorphic conditions responsible for producing blueschists were restricted in time. Many blueschists are found at high levels in orogenic belts, and older occurrences could have been removed by post-orogenic erosion (which is usually rapid and intense owing to uplift of the mountain chain). Alternatively, the minerals in blueschists could have been replaced by other minerals during a later, high-temperature metamorphic event. There is some evidence for this in the case of blueschists from the Alps. The high-pressure minerals of blueschists are susceptible to recrystallisation and replacement by other minerals at higher temperatures and lower pressures. The tectonic significance of blueschists will be referred to again in Chapter 5.

Summary

In Chapter 4 examples of regional metamorphism in Precambrian shields and younger fold mountain belts and blueschist metamorphism in subduction zones were presented.

The example quoted of regional metamorphism in an orogenic belt was the Dalradian rocks of Scotaland, with its progressive sequence of zones (Barrow's zones) with characteristic index minerals, i.e. chlorite → biotite → garnet → staurolite → kyanite → sillimanite, from low to high grade. A small part of the Dalradian is characterised by the sequence, in pelitic rocks also: chlorite → biotite → cordierite → andalusite → sillimanite. These are the Buchan zones, which arose due to low-pressure–high-temperature metamorphism. Textural changes also occur during metamorphism, giving the sequence shale → slate → phyllite → schist → gneiss, in pelitic sediments.

The metamorphic rocks of Precambrian shields are typically banded gneisses of granitic composition and small amounts of high-pressure granulites and metasediments, which may show low metamorphic grades. Granulites often occur in the oldest parts of shields; they are rocks with granoblastic textures and anhydrous minerals. It is thought that water, driven off during the metamorphism of granulites, migrated upwards and played a role in the formation of banded gneisses which contain abundant hydrated silicates. Banded gneisses were probably originally plutonic and volcanic igneous rocks. Migmatites and granitic intrusions are common in shields. Migmatites are mixed rocks, formed by partial melting in which granitic material has invaded a host rock of high metamorphic grade and non-granitic composition. Partial melting occurs in metamorphic situations when the quartz and feldspar components of rocks of suitable composition melt in the presence of water at around 750 °C to produce a wet granitic melt, leaving behind a still-solid, more basic material.

Blueschists are restricted in time to young orogenic belts and in space to subduction zone environments. They form owing to unusually high pressures, low temperatures and low geothermal gradients, where sediments are metamorphosed above a lithospheric slab that is descending into the upper mantle.

Exercises

1   A pyroxene–feldspar gneiss is folded and metamorphosed during a second metamorphic event at a lower grade and with the introduction of water. What minerals might be expected to develop? Suggest a name for the resulting rock. What term is used for this type of metamorphism?

2   Draw a pair of axes to represent pressure and temperature. Indicate the approximate

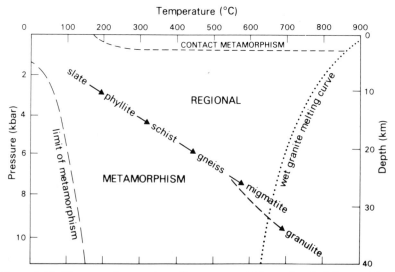

Figure 4.19   Pressure–temperature diagram on which are located the positions where conditions are suitable to produce slate, etc. from pelitic sediments.

positions of slate, phyllite, schist and gneiss on the diagram. Mark in the positon occupied by contact metamorphism. Compare your diagram with Figure 4.19.

3 Match mineral assemblages (a) to (e) with rock names (1) to (7):

(a) quartz + mica + garnet   (1) marble
(b) hornblende + epidote + calcite   (2) quartzite
(c) pyroxene + plagioclase   (3) amphibolite
(d) quartz   (4) banded gneiss
(e) pyroxene + garnet   (5) garnet–mica schist
                                       (6) granulite
                                       (7) eclogite

4 Give the metamorphic equivalents of the following:

(a) muddy limestone, metamorphosed at medium grade;
(b) basalt, metamorphosed at high grade;
(c) shale, metamorphosed at medium grade.

5 Suggest possible mineral assemblages that might develop in the rocks in the above exercise, at the appropriate metamorphic grades.

5 Mountain building and metamorphic rocks

Mountain belts, or orogenic belts, are long, narrow, gently curved features on the Earth's crust, usually with prominent relief. Old mountain belts have a lower average elevation than younger belts because of erosion. Metamorphic rocks are closely associated with mountain belts, especially those on continents. Old, deeply eroded mountain chains have more metamorphic rocks exposed at the surface than do younger chains. Metamorphism occurs deeply within a mountain chain as it is formed by folding and compression. If you squeeze a piece of plasticine, it will become thinner and wider, but the volume will remain the same. Mountain belts arise by compressive forces causing a shortening of the crust. The Earth's crust is greatly thickened in mountain chains, e.g. in the Himalayas it is over 80 km thick, compared with a continental average of 35–40 km. High mountain chains are subject to uplift and rapid erosion, leading to the eventual exposure of metamorphic rocks in their cores.

The Earth's crust is made up of a number of tectonic plates which fit together like a mosaic, or rather like the pieces of a shell (Fig. 5.1). Metamorphic rocks are found in the Precambrian shields of continental plates and in fold mountain belts around certain plate margins. The plate margins of concern to us are the collision zones between two continental plates or between an oceanic plate and a continental plate.

Continental collision zones

Figure 5.1 shows the plate collision zones of the world and the fold mountain chains found there. Asia and Europe meet along the line of the Urals; Africa meets Eurasia along the vast chain of the Alps, Carpathians and Himalayas; the Caledonian mountain chain is an old collision zone between the North American and Eurasian plates. A more obvious picture emerges if the positions of America and Europe are reconstructed before the opening of the Atlantic Ocean (Fig. 5.2). The Hercynian belt of Europe is now a highly fragmented orogenic belt that resulted from the collision of Africa with Europe. This belt is older than the Alps, having developed at about the same time as the Ural mountains (i.e. some 250–300 Ma ago).

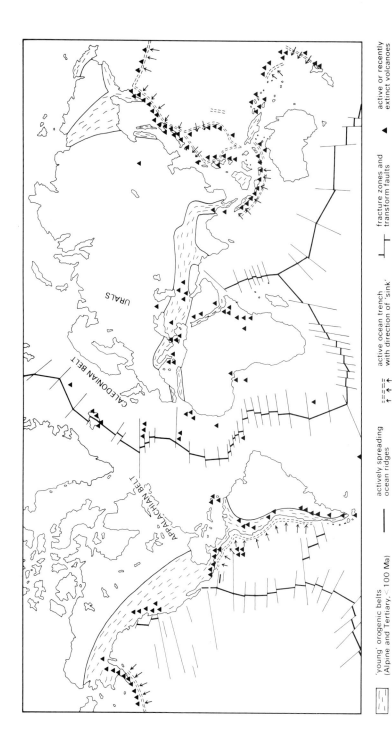

Figure 5.1 **Lithospheric plates and old collision zones.** The Earth's crust is comprised of several large rigid plates which are able to move, by spreading outwards away from the mid-ocean ridges. Plate boundaries are of three types: (a) ocean–ocean – 'conservative', transform faults; (b) ocean–continent – 'destructive', ocean disappears in trench; (c) continent–continent – 'collision', young mountain belts.

⸗⸗	'young' orogenic belts (Alpine and Tertiary, <100 Ma)
——	actively spreading ocean ridges
⋹⋹⋹ ↑↑↑	active ocean trench with direction of 'sink'
⊥	fracture zones and transform faults
▲	active or recently extinct volcanoes

URALS

CALEDONIAN BELT

APPALACHIAN BELT

Figure 5.2   Reconstruction of the geology of the North Atlantic province before continental break-up and drifting.

In all these cases, orogenic belts developed as continental plates were driven towards each other. The intervening oceanic crust was gradually subducted beneath the continental masses. Eventually the continents collided and the ocean between was closed. Continental crust is not subducted into the mantle because it has a lower density than the mantle. Instead, sedimentary basins on continental margins are folded, compressed and deformed into mountain chains where two continents collide. The crust becomes shortened and thickened along the collision zone. In the case of the Himalayas, the crust has been doubled in thickness due to a combination of folding and thrusting, with many nappe folds being piled one on top of the other along thrust faults (see also the section on the Moine Thrust Zone, p. 61). This thickened crust is pushed down into the hot upper mantle, which is a contributory factor to the high heat flow in orogenic belts (see Table 2.4). The other contribution to high heat flow comes from the sediments themselves, which contain minerals with radioactive elements. Pressure due to depth of burial, high strain due to compression, and high temperatures and heat flow are responsible for metamorphism in orogenic belts. Partial melting (p. 88) may take place near the base of the thickened crust leading to the formation of granitic magmas, which move upwards and intrude rocks that are being folded and metamorphosed. The sketches in Figure 5.3 illustrate a possible sequence of events in the evolution of the Caledonian chain in Britain as a continent/ocean collision zone.

Original rock types in continental collision-zone environments are highly varied, ranging from pelitic mudstones and shales through quartz-rich sediments that include sandstones, arkoses and greywackes. Carbonate sediments also occur, and volcanic rocks are usually present. It will be argued later (p. 106) that continental collision is preceded by the subduction of oceanic crust, so that these collision zones are sites of calc-alkaline magmatism (intrusive and extrusive igneous rocks of continental regions, forming the basalt–andesite–dacite–rhyolite suite), the products of which are incorporated into the continental crust and become involved in deformation and metamorphism. This great diversity of rock types in these collision zones means that a wide range of metamorphic rocks will be produced during an orogeny at such a site.

Pressure and temperature conditions and geothermal gradients in continental collision zones vary a great deal, with the result that all combinations of low-, medium- and high-pressure and temperature metamorphism are possible. Some orogenic belts are characterised by medium heat flow, with Barrow-type metamorphic zones developed (see p. 67). Others have high heat flow and show Buchan-type zones (p. 67). Patches of blueschists and eclogites (pp. 92–93), indicating low-temperature, low-heat-flow, high-pressure metamorphism, are found throughout certain orogenic belts, such as the Alps and Himalayas.

The Caledonian–Appalachian belt stretches from Greenland and northern Norway through Scotland via the Shetland Isles, then south-westwards into Wales, Ireland and the eastern seaboard of North America, where it again becomes NE–SW in orientation (Fig. 5.4). The

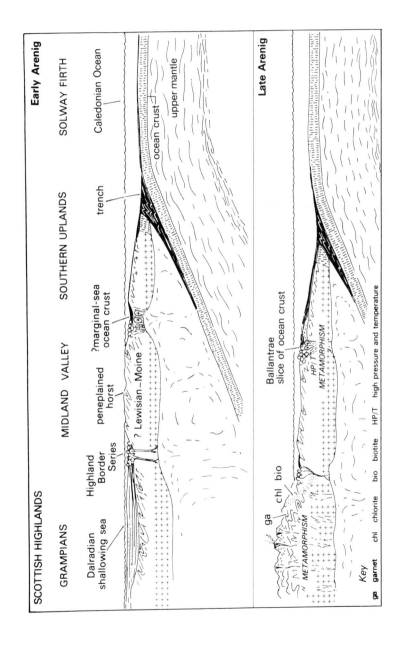

SCOTTISH HIGHLANDS

Early Arenig

GRAMPIANS   MIDLAND VALLEY   SOUTHERN UPLANDS   SOLWAY FIRTH

Dalradian shallowing sea

Highland Border Series

peneplained horst   ?marginal-sea ocean crust   trench   Caledonian Ocean

? Lewisian–Moine   ocean crust   upper mantle

Late Arenig

Ballantrae slice of ocean crust

HP/T METAMORPHISM

ga chl bio

METAMORPHISM

Key

ga garnet   chl chlorite   bio biotite   HP/T high pressure and temperature

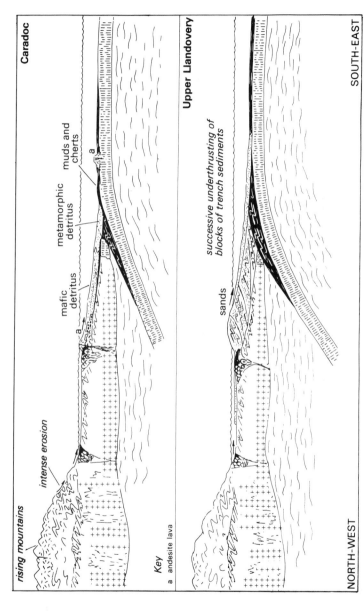

Figure 5.3 Possible sequence of events in the evolution of the Caledonian belt as a continent/ocean collision zone.

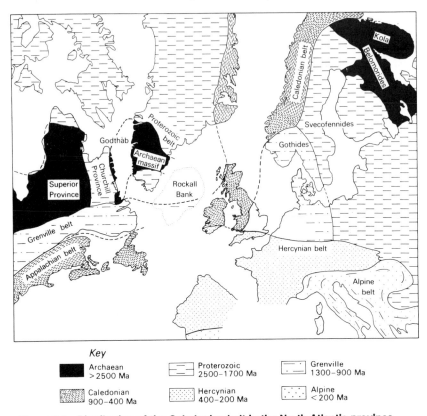

Key

■ Archaean >2500 Ma	☰ Proterozoic 2500–1700 Ma	⊡ Grenville 1300–900 Ma
▨ Caledonian 900–400 Ma	⊡ Hercynian 400–200 Ma	⊡ Alpine <200 Ma

Figure 5.4   **Distribution of the Caledonian belt in the North Atlantic province.**

southern margin of the belt is abruptly marked by the edge of the Hercynian belt (see Fig. 5.4). In Britain the Caledonian fold belt is divided into a northern zone (the Scottish Highlands), a central zone (the Southern Uplands of Scotland and the English Lake District) and a southern zone (Wales and Anglesey) (Fig. 5.5). Metamorphism in the Scottish Highlands was of the medium-pressure, medium-temperature type over most of the region, although the Buchan area (Fig. 4.5) shows high-temperature–low-pressure metamorphism. Thick sediments, the Dalradian and Moine rocks, were metamorphosed to slates, schists, gneisses, migmatites, quartzites, marbles and amphibolites. The rocks were deformed several times during the Caledonian orogeny. Tempera-. tures rose gradually during folding, and metamorphism reached a peak in early Ordovician times. Sillimanite occurs in the Buchan area of north-east Scotland in an area of migmatites and it may have been

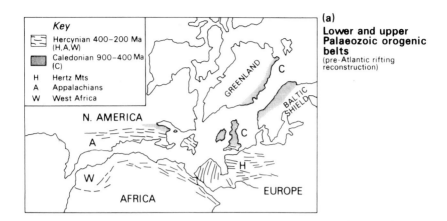

(a)
Lower and upper Palaeozoic orogenic belts
(pre-Atlantic rifting reconstruction)

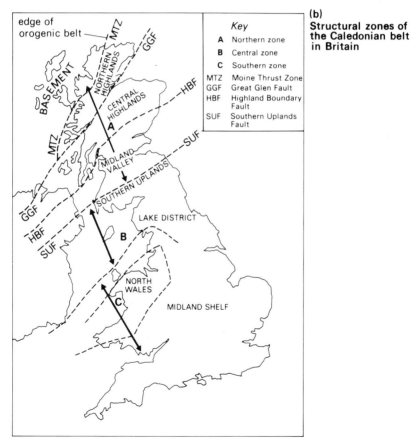

(b)
Structural zones of the Caledonian belt in Britain

Figure 5.5 Zones of the Caledonian orogenic belt in the British Isles.

produced by a local rise in temperature. The sillimanite zone (one of the Buchan zones, p. 71) is narrow (Fig. 4.5). Granites are widespread in the Scottish Highlands (Fig. 4.9) and they occur in two age groups. The older granites are about 500 Ma old and they formed roughly at the same time as the folding and metamorphism of the thick sediments. These are described as syntectonic granites, meaning that they formed by partial melting during deformation. Some of them were subsequently deformed to produce granitic gneisses and augen gneisses. Granites also formed at around 400 Ma ago, after the peak of metamorphism and deformation. These younger granites are called post-tectonic and they often have contact aureoles associated with them. They are not deformed, in contrast to the older group.

In the Southern Uplands of Scotland and in the English Lake District, the metamorphic rocks are of quite a different character from those in the Scottish Highlands. The grade of metamorphism is low, with strongly cleaved slates being typical. Original features of sedimentary and volcanic origin are frequently preserved. There is some evidence that metamorphism in the central zone of the Caledonian belt was high-pressure–low-temperature in nature, at least in parts of the zone. The rocks are Ordovician to Silurian in age and they consist of a thick pile of volcanics, shales, cherts and greywackes. In the southern zone, Precambrian rocks occur in Anglesey, the Welsh borders and sporadically elsewhere. Serpentinites and blueschists occur, indicating high-pressure–low-temperature metamorphism of basic igneous rocks. Cambrian to Silurian sediments overlie these rocks unconformably. They are shales and turbidites (muddy sediments transported by rapidly flowing submarine turbidity currents), which were deformed and metamorphosed at very low grade, producing mainly slates.

The evolution of the Caledonian–Appalachian orogenic belt is considered to be as follows. Sediments were deposited in an ocean basin during late Precambrian (1000 Ma ago) to Ordovician time. Thin sediments accumulated on a shallow-water shelf, followed outwards (oceanwards) by thick clastic sediments in deep troughs or sedimentary basins. The Ordovician ocean floor was covered by deep-water sediments, thin black muds and cherts. As the North American and European plates were pushed towards one another, the ocean gradually closed and was progressively subducted under the continents. This gave rise to high-pressure–low-temperature, low-heat-flow metamorphism above the subduction zones. Eventually, by Silurian times, the ocean was much narrower, and thick greywackes and siltstones covered its floor. By the Devonian, the ocean was completely closed and continental collision had occurred. The sediments in the northern zone were metamorphosed under medium-pressure and medium- to high-temperature conditions. Partial melting of the lower crust resulted in the formation of granitic magmas, which moved upwards and intruded rocks at higher levels. Caledonian orogenic activity ended during the Devonian with the intrusion of post-orogenic granites. Finally, the fold belt underwent uplift and deep erosion. The orogenic cycle was complete: sedimentation, folding, thrusting, metamorphism, granitic intrusion, uplift, stabilisation and erosion had taken place.

Continent/ocean collision zones

Metamorphic rocks are found in belts along continental margins, such as those that occur down the west coast of North and South America (Fig. 5.6). In South America the Pacific Ocean Plate is presently being thrust under the continent along a subduction zone. Metamorphic

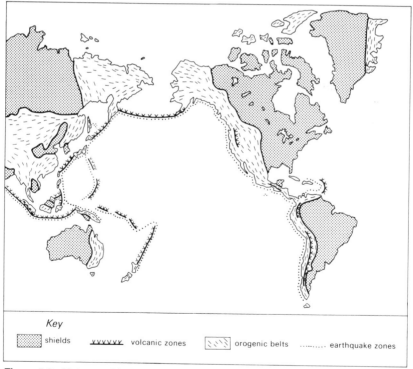

Key

▒ shields   ᵥᵥᵥᵥᵥᵥ volcanic zones   [⟍⟍⟍] orogenic belts   ·········· earthquake zones

Figure 5.6   Metamorphic belts in the circum-Pacific region.

belts of late Palaeozoic age in Chile run parallel to the Pacific margin, whereas the cordillera of North America is of Mesozoic age and contains the Franciscan and Sierra Nevada metamorphic belts (p. 93). Enormous granite batholiths are a common feature of the Sierra Nevada and they account for much of the mountain chain.

Belts of metamorphic rocks have formed under island arcs, such as those in Japan, New Zealand, the Kurile Islands and Sakhalin in the Pacific Ocean (Fig. 5.6). Island arcs are chains of volcanically active oceanic islands, producing large amounts of acid and intermediate igneous rocks at the surface. Metamorphic belts beneath island arcs formed by the underthrusting of the Pacific Ocean plate in the direction of surrounding continental plates.

High-pressure–low-temperature metamorphism is typical of rocks metamorphosed in subduction zones, as explained previously (p. 108). Geothermal gradients in these environments are 10 °C per kilometre, which is very low. The reason for this is that cold slabs of crust are being dragged down into the hot mantle, so that surfaces of equal temperature dip down (Fig. 5.7). High-pressure metamorphism results from compressive forces where an ocean plate collides with a continental plate, producing metamorphic rocks with low grades.

Greywackes (mixed clastic sediments, usually in thick wedge-shaped

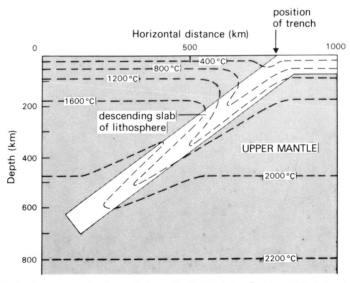

Figure 5.7   Arrangement of geotherms down a subduction zone. The geotherms appear to dip down with the cold slab of crust being subducted.

piles) are the most abundant rock types in continent/ocean collision zones, with pelitic sediments being relatively rare. Regional metamorphic rocks are arranged in a sequence of parallel belts or zones, reflecting their formation at successively greater depths in the crust. The zones are:

zeolite-bearing rocks	5–10 km depth of burial
blueschists ⎫	
greenschists ⎬	35–40 km depth of burial
amphibolites ⎭	

This metamorphic sequence is seen in the Franciscan area of western California (Fig. 4.17). The metamorphic event at about 150 Ma ago produced the blueschists. Because of the low heat flow, high-pressure metamorphic belts are not usually accompanied by granites. In the case of the Franciscan rocks, greywackes were probably deposited directly onto oceanic crust, i.e. a granitic-type continental basement to the greywackes was absent. Rocks of the Californian part of the cordillera are highly deformed, with folding, faulting and thrusting having produced a complicated sequence of rocks that includes the metamorphosed equivalents of slices of oceanic crust.

Large granitic batholiths form an important part of the American cordillera all the way from Alaska to Chile. The most prominent are the Coast Range, Idaho, Sierra Nevada, California and Peruvian batholiths (Fig. 5.6). Each major batholith may have a large number of smaller plutons in the complex, with hundreds of small 'bubbles' of granite making up a large mass. Some of the batholiths are immense, being 1500 km long by 200 km wide. Although they are referred to as being of 'granite', the batholiths are actually composed mostly of granodiorite. (The abundant banded gneisses in Precambrian shields are of this composition.) These large batholiths were intruded at fairly shallow depths of 5–10 km and have contact aureoles, which were superimposed on regionally metamorphosed and deformed sediments and volcanic rocks. In such cases, contact metamorphism is said to 'overprint' regional metamorphism. The volcanic rocks are andesites and rhyolites, of the same composition as the plutonic rocks which have intruded them. Gneisses of this composition are present in some of the deeply eroded batholiths of the cordilleran mountain chain in South America. The intrusive rocks were emplaced in several distinct phases. Synorogenic (or syntectonic) granitic rocks were emplaced four times, between 200 Ma and 100 Ma ago, while post-orogenic (or post-tectonic) plutons were intruded two or three times, from 70 Ma to 10 Ma ago. This vast

amount of acidic magma seems to have been produced by partial melting at the base of a thick crust during an orogenic episode. The continental crust beneath the present day Sierra Nevada is 50 km thick.
Metamorphism was of the high-temperature–low-pressure type with
high heat flow, which is consistent with the large amount of granitic
magma. It may be that the American cordillera consists of a **pair** of
metamorphic belts. Near the Pacific margin is the high-pressure–low-
temperature half of the pair with its blueschists, in the Franciscan area
of California. This is matched in the Sierra Nevada, on the continental side, where the high-temperature, high-heat-flow, low-pressure
metamorphic belt occurs together with the Sierra Nevada granitic
batholith. The American cordillera has many important mineral
deposits associated with the igneous rocks, iron, copper, gold, silver,
lead and zinc being a few of the metals present. Metallogenic provinces
are arranged in parallel alignment with the orogenic belt.

The reason for the existence of the paired metamorphic belts seems
to be that the Pacific Ocean plate is being thrust under the North and
South American continental plates. Blueschists occur at the continental
margin, whereas gneisses and granites are found inland, in the interior.
This reflects the increasing depth of the subduction zone away from the
continent–ocean margin (see Figs 2.11, 4.18, 5.3 & 7).

Metamorphic belts through time

Heat flow through the continental crust has not been constant in geological time. Instead, there has been a decrease with time, as a result of
which there are different kinds of regional metamorphic rocks around
the world in rocks of various ages. Low- and medium-pressure
metamorphic belts are found from the Precambrian to the Tertiary.

Table 5.1 Abundances (in %) of major rock types in continental crustal provinces.

Rock type	Archaean cores	Precambrian fold belts	Phanerozoic fold belts
granite and granodiorite	15	15	30
gneiss and migmatite	60	65	10
granulite	7	7	—
amphibolite and schist	5	5	—
sediments	—	6	47
volcanics	11	1	13
basic–ultrabasic rocks	2	2	—

High-pressure belts, on the other hand, seem to have formed only since the end of the Precambrian, most being Mesozoic to Cenozoic in age (but see p. 93 for a discussion of this point). A few Palaeozoic examples of blueschists are found in the Caledonian belt of Scotland and Ireland, and in the Ural mountains of the USSR. Geothermal gradients in the Precambrian may have been too steep to allow these high-pressure–low-temperature metamorphic belts to form. Outcrops of high-pressure–high-temperature granulites and pyroxene gneisses are largely restricted to areas of Precambrian rocks and form parts of the cores of shields (Table 5.1).

Heat flow with time

Certain geothermal gradients seem to be characteristic of different stages in the Earth's evolution. Since the Precambrian there has been a steady decrease in heat production and in average thermal gradients, owing to the decrease in heat-producing isotopes as they decay. Note the use of the word 'average' here, since heat flow and geothermal gradients need not have been average during mountain building. In fact, heat flow can be quite abnormal, as much depends on the thickness of the crust through time. For example, the continental crust *may* have been thinner (but not by much) in the early Precambrian than at present, and tectonic activity *may* have proceeded faster then also; we are not really sure.

Using the compositions of the pyroxenes and feldspars in granulites from the Lewisian Complex, it has been calculated that the rocks could have formed only if the crust had been about 40 km thick during the Archaean. Since these rocks are now exposed at the surface and are underlain by other rocks, the Precambrian crust must have been fairly thick, and possibly not much different to the thickness in modern orogenic belts. The overall effect of a thinner crust and accelerated tectonic activity in the Precambrian would have been to produce lower pressures and steeper thermal gradients. In consequence, blueschist metamorphism (high pressure, low temperature) could not have occurred. It has already been pointed out that blueschists are completely absent from early Precambrian rocks, but there are other possible explanations for this absence (p. 94). Geothermal gradients have varied in time and from place to place. The general decrease in gradients from the early Precambrian to the present was related to a decrease in radioactive heat. Heat generated by the radioactive decay of potassium-40 and uranium was several times what it is today. Examine Figure 5.8 and

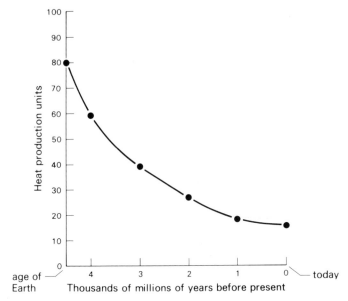

Figure 5.8   Graph showing change in heat production with time.

note the steep decline of the curve. A curve with the sort of shape of Figure 5.8 is described as **exponential**. Curves which represent heat flow, heat production, heat loss, radioactive decay, etc. are exponential in shape (refer back to Figs 2.1, 2.2 & 3.1).

Evolution of the Earth's crust

Continental growth largely took place in three main stages during Earth history, in the following periods:

(a) Archaean (early Precambrian, 4600–2500 Ma ago),
(b) Proterozoic (late Precambrian, 2500–600 Ma ago),
(c) Phanerozoic (post-Precambrian, 600–0 Ma ago).

Continents first appeared in the Archaean possibly as small plates, which eventually converged to form larger continents. These early continents gradually thickened and enlarged during the Archaean. All exposed rocks of Archaean age in shields are metamorphic, reflecting the removal of the upper Archaean crust that once overlayed them. In many instances these ancient metamorphic rocks still preserve original sedimentary and volcanic features, such as cross bedding, ripple marks, pillow structure and vesicular structure (Fig. 5.9). Tectonic activity then may have been more marked, i.e. orogenic cycles were completed relatively more rapidly than in more recent periods of Earth history. By the Proterozoic the continents were stabilised and about three-quarters of the present area and volume of continents had formed by about 2500 Ma ago. Stable Precambrian crustal blocks are referred to as cratons. Cratons have suffered little or no deformation since the Precambrian. Modern plate tectonic activity probably became established during the Proterozoic. The Phanerozoic was a period of Earth history when large continents broke up, drifted apart and collided. Mountain chains and metamorphic belts formed in collision zones and progressively younger orogenic belts attached themselves to the Precambrian cores or cratons. Thus the continents grew outwards as sedimentary basins around the cratons were closed and compressed. Mountain belts containing metamorphic rocks and granitic intrusions then developed at continental margins. This concentric arrangement of orogenic belts is best seen in North America (Fig. 4.14). The relative deceleration of tectonic activity since the Archaean is related to heat flow. Heat energy is the driving force of the Earth's activity, and heat generation generally declined during the Proterozoic.

Metamorphic rocks and the early history of the Earth

The great majority of the Earth's continental crust was produced during the Precambrian. The Precambrian constitutes 88% of geological time. Archaean rocks are mostly metamorphic, but in the case of Proterozoic rocks there are many examples around the world of undeformed, nonmetamorphic platform sediments lying on Archaean basement. There are also, of course, many examples of Proterozoic metamorphic rocks.

A fundamental event in the history of the Earth was the formation of the continental crust. Continental crust, unlike oceanic crust, is not destroyed by subduction into the mantle, but it increases in total volume with time. Thus the creation of the continents was an irreversible event. The Earth is in continual motion, a fact which means that many events and processes proceed in one direction only. It has already been pointed out that total heat production has decreased with time (p. 111). More heat-producing isotopes were present after the birth of the Earth, 4600 Ma ago, than today. The Earth's internal heat is the energy source responsible for much of the planet's activity. In the next sections we shall look briefly at the consequences of this, in particular to see if modern plate tectonic theory can be applied to the Precambrian. In so doing, some knowledge of the metamorphic structure of Precambrian shields will be gained.

Figure 5.9 Bedding structures. Original bedding structures in practically unmetamorphosed Precambrian rocks, over 2000 Ma old, from the Baltic Shield (Finnish and Soviet Karelia). (a) cross-bedded sandstone (now quartzite), (b) linguloid (tongue-shaped) ripple marks on the bedding surface of a sandstone, (c) ropy surface of basaltic lava.

Figure 5.9 – *continued.*

The Archaean. Precambrian shields consist of rocks formed in two different metamorphic environments. There are, first, the so-called **greenstone belts** which have been deformed and metamorphosed at relatively low grades and, secondly, the contrasting gneiss terrains which are made up of granulites, granitic gneisses and migmatites. The gneisses of these high-grade terrains were intensely deformed and recrystallised at moderate to high pressures and temperatures. This is only a *general* pattern, for there are parts of shields in which greenstones, granitic rocks and gneisses are gradational (with transitional rock types and metamorphic grades) and are not easily separable.

Greenstone belts are long, narrow synforms containing thick sequences of metamorphosed basaltic lavas and overlying sediments. The belts were invaded by granitic intrusions and are separated by intervening regions of granitic gneiss (Fig. 5.10). Greenstone belts are known from most Precambrian shields, but the Scottish shield fragment is too small and the Greenland Shield has its interior covered by ice, so it is not known if there are any greenstone belts in these areas. The belts formed in most continents during the period 2800–2600 Ma ago. There are three major stratigraphic units in all the belts:

(a) upper group: greywackes, conglomerates, sandstones, banded iron-
        stones,

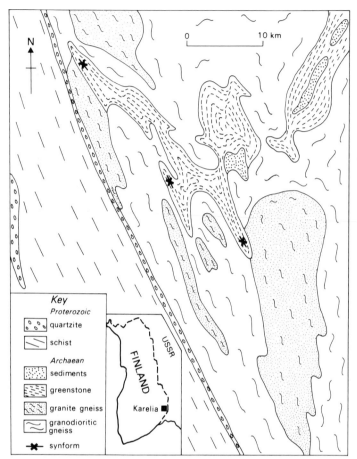

Figure 5.10   Greenstone belt in the Precambrian basement of Karelia, East Finland.

(b) central group: andesitic volcanic rocks,
(c) lower group: basic to ultrabasic lavas.

Ultrabasic lavas were first described from the Archaean, but are now known to occur in younger settings. They were probably derived from the mantle by high degrees of melting. These lavas are unusual in being richer in magnesium than are modern lavas of the ocean floor, that are also derived by partial melting of the upper mantle. Chemical studies of these metamorphosed ultrabasic lavas indicate that they were derived from the early mantle during a thermal episode when it was extensively melted. Lavas occurring higher in the sequence in greenstone belts are basalt, andesite and dacite, similar in composition to lavas of modern island arcs (p. 110). Sediments found in the upper group are mostly immature clastics, i.e. greywackes and conglomerates. The clastic material was derived from nearby granitic gneisses and volcanic rocks by rapid erosion, transport and deposition.

The cycle of greenstone belt formation ended with the folding and metamorphism of the lavas and sediments. Typical minerals in the low-grade metamorphosed lavas are chlorite (in greenschist) and amphibole (in amphibolite). During this deformational episode, the greenstone belts were intruded by granitic magmas. Some of the granitic bodies were then highly deformed themselves. Greenstone belts are often the sites of mineralisation, e.g. economic deposits of copper, nickel, chromium, gold and silver occur in Canada and South Africa in such belts. Some of the sedimentary banded iron formations are also of economic significance. Figure 5.11 shows folded banded ironstones from a greenstone belt in Karelia, eastern Finland (Fig. 5.10).

Greenstone belts are thought to represent the Precambrian equivalent of younger **marginal basins**. Several marginal basins are found down the west coast of North and South America, on the continental side of the cordillera. They were originally downwarps in the crust on the landward side of the young mountains. As a result of the collision of the Pacific Ocean plate with the American continental plates, the marginal basins were closed, compressed and deformed, and their rocks metamorphosed. There are many similarities between the rock types in marginal basins and Archaean greenstone belts. Large amounts of coarse, immature clastic sediments are derived from the high mountains of the cordillera. Andesitic volcanism and granitic intrusions are well known features of marginal basins, and oceanic-type basalt lavas occur nearby.

High-grade Archaean granulite–gneiss belts are found in many shield areas. Most were metamorphosed in the period 2700–3100 Ma ago, and these high-grade belts sometimes contain the oldest rocks in a region. Belts older than this occur in Greenland, Labrador and Zimbabwe. The granulite–gneiss belts generally consist of three highly metamorphosed rock suites:

(a) quartzite, mica schists with kyanite and sillimanite, and metamorphosed basic rocks, 5%;
(b) quartzo-feldspathic gneiss (granodioritic), 85%;
(c) basic and ultrabasic layered igneous intrusions, fragments only.

These three suites need not always form separate, distinct tracts, e.g. in Greenland (a) and (b) are interleaved, enclaves of (c) occur in (b), and

Figure 5.11   Folds in banded ironstones, Karelia, Finland.

entire sheets of (c) have intruded (b). In suite (a), the presence of
aluminosilicates in kyanite schists and sillimanite gneisses indicates original shaly sediments. Associated rocks are marbles and quartzites. These
metasediments form thin, discontinuous schist horizons among the
gneisses, and account for a small proportion of the total volume of rocks

in an area. Basic to ultrabasic metamorphosed igneous rocks (c) occur in association with the metasediments. The igneous rocks are highly deformed, with once-continuous thick sheets broken up into lenses, pods and boudins (sausage-shaped blocks), then interleaved with the schists and gneisses soon after they crystallised. The dominant rock type of high-grade terrains is (b), pale coloured banded quartzo-feldspathic gneiss, containing plagioclase, quartz, hornblende and biotite. The overall (bulk) chemical composition of the gneisses is granodioritic. Huge batholiths with this composition are found in great abundance in the Andes and in the cordillera on the west coast of North America. Deeply eroded portions of these young fold mountain belts consist of granodiorite that has been metamorphosed to banded gneiss. It is possible, then, that the high-grade gneiss terrains of shield areas may represent deeply eroded and highly metamorphosed granodiorites. The tectonic environment in which these rocks formed could have been similar to a more recent cordillera, situated above a subduction zone. Large volumes of granodioritic magma are produced in such environments.

Granulites are found as remnants in the central portions of Archaean shields. They are the products of high-pressure–high-temperature metamorphism of dry rocks and were formed in the deepest parts of the continental crust (35–40 km). Many granulites around the world show an age of metamorphism in the period 2800–2600 Ma.

The boundary between the Archaean and the Proterozoic is put at 2500 Ma. From the graph in Figure 5.8 the heat production at 3500 Ma and 2500 Ma was 50 hpu and 30 hpu respectively, i.e. heat production decreased markedly during the Archaean (where 0.418×10^{-6} hpu = 1.0 W m^{-3}). The Archaean/Proterozoic boundary is of major significance in the evolution of the Earth, marking the change from the creation of many small continental plates and plate collision episodes to larger, thicker, more stable plates in the Proterozoic. This changeover is not likely to have occurred rapidly, nor everywhere at the same time. Instead, a transition period lasting 300–400 Ma seems probable.

The Proterozoic. Compared to the Archaean, the Proterozoic was a period of Earth history when earlier-formed rocks were repeatedly deformed and metamorphosed. The Archaean, in contrast, represents a period when entirely new continental crust was created. Proterozoic tectonic activity was characterised by two major episodes of mountain building at 1800 Ma and 1000 Ma ago (Table 5.2). Swarms of basic dykes are common at the margins of Proterozoic belts. The main trends of folds and foliations tend to run parallel to the dyke swarms.

Table 5.2 Major events in the early evolution of the crust.

	Age (Ma)	Tectonic event
Proterozoic	750	collision-type orogenic belts
	1000	Grenville–Moine collision belt
	1500	granite intrusion
	1800–2100	early Proterozoic orogenic belts
	2150	uplift and erosion
	2200	intrusion of basic dyke swarms
	2500	formation of thick, stable continents
Archaean	2700–3800	origin and growth of small continental plates with granulite–gneiss belts and granite–greenstone belts
	3800–4200	meteorite impact cratering
	4500	origin of the Earth

Proterozoic deformation and metamorphism were intense, with sediments in deep basins becoming gneisses. Major thrusts and folds indicate that the crust suffered intense compression some 1800 Ma ago. The basic dykes became deformed and flattened, with original olivine and pyroxene in the dolerites being replaced by hornblende during metamorphism. Intense deformation resulted in the dykes taking on strong directional fabrics – foliation and lineation – becoming amphibolites and hornblende schists. The occurrence of granitic gneisses and migmatites and the absence of granulites imply that water was present during the metamorphism.

The Grenville orogenic belt is a 1000 Ma old linear belt of folded metamorphic rocks in southern Canada and southern Norway. The belt has many similarities to younger fold mountain chains and is thought to represent the deeply eroded equivalent of a Himalayan-type continent/continent collision zone. High-temperature metamorphism and partial melting of the lower crust, resulting in the production of igneous rocks, were characteristic features of the Grenville orogeny. Fragments of the Grenville orogenic belt are found within the younger Caledonian belt in Scotland and the west of Ireland. Here, rocks formed in the Grenville orogeny were affected by Caledonian events, and Caledonian metamorphism has overprinted Grenvillian metamorphism. It is evident that, by the start of the Proterozoic, tectonic activity had developed a pattern that was to be maintained for much of the rest of geological time, i.e. sedimentary basins developed around continental margins, with these basins later becoming the sites of fold mountain chains during continental collisions. The tectonic environment was one of plate movement and collision, resulting in the continents growing by the addition of successive fold belts around central Archaean cores.

The question arises: did plate tectonic processes operate in the Archaean? The answer seems to be yes, but on a different scale from plate tectonics in later periods of Earth history. The larger amount of heat energy available during the Archaean was used to fuel tectonic activity at a faster rate than subsequently. Had this not been the case, the heat would have resulted in widespread complete melting of the crust at shallow depths, for which there appears to be no evidence.

The picture emerging as the result of recent research is of a rapidly cooling Earth with several small continental crustal plates and large oceanic (basaltic) plates. These microcontinents moved faster and collided more frequently in the Archaean than in more recent times. Basaltic crust was consumed down low-angled subduction zones beneath the microcontinents, resulting in intense flattening of the continental rocks and the production of granodioritic magmas by partial melting. There is a complex relationship between igneous intrusion, deformation and high-grade regional metamorphism. Low-angled subduction resulted in partial melting over geographically extensive areas, with granitic material moving upwards and forming broad belts of intrusive rocks. In the Archaean low-grade metamorphic belts, large numbers of granitic and granodioritic batholiths occur between greenstone belts. The forceful intrusion of dome-shaped granitic bodies was responsible in part for deforming the greenstone belts, by squashing them.

Listed below are the irreversible events in the early history of the Earth that occurred once only and which provided a framework for the later evolution of the crust:

(1) the formation of the Earth;
(2) meteorite impact cratering;
(3) cooling and formation of earliest crust;
(4) formation of microcontinental crustal plates;
(5) rapid movement, collision and welding together of several small continents to form a few large ones;
(6) consolidation of Precambrian crust and development of linear fold mountain belts at continental margins.

The total area and volume of continental crust can only grow bigger, since the granitic material of which they are built is not destroyed by subduction. In several respects the Theory of Uniformitarianism (usually expressed in the aphorism 'the present is the key to the past') does not apply to events in the early history of the Earth. Rather, the past may provide us with the key to modern plate motions.

Summary

Mountain belts are gently curved, narrow zones of the crust, composed of sedimentary and volcanic rocks deformed by strong compression, resulting in the shortening and thickening of the crust. They contain metamorphic and plutonic igneous rocks at depth and mostly occur along the sites of continent/continent and continent/ocean plate collision zones.

Precambrian time is divided into Archaean (4600–2500 Ma) and Proterozoic (2500–600 Ma). The Archaean represents a unique period in Earth history in terms of tectonic processes. Archaean continental crust has two types of metamorphic belt, high-grade granulite–gneiss terrains and low-grade granite–greenstone belts. Greenstone belts, which formed in the period 2600–2800 Ma ago, consist of ultrabasic lavas, andesites and immature clastic sediments. They were folded into synforms and were intruded by granitic magmas. Granulite–gneiss belts crystallised at 2700–3100 Ma ago. They consist of acidic gneiss, thin metasediments and fractured remnants of large ultrabasic to basic igneous intrusions. The pattern of Archaean tectonics was dominated by small continental plates moving and colliding at a faster rate than today, owing mainly to the much greater heat energy available. High-grade and low-grade belts represent crustal sections of varying depth through Andean-type collision zones.

The Proterozoic saw the establishment of larger, more stable continental plates with marginal fold mountain belts. Most of the Earth's crust had formed by the Proterozoic. Tectonic activity in the Proterozoic resembled that in younger geological periods. Fold belts and metamorphic zones originated by a mechanism that would imply Alpine–Himalayan type collision zones.

Exercises

1   Mid-oceanic ridges have not been mentioned in this chapter. Would you describe them as mountain belts? How do they differ from continental mountain belts?
2   Draw a sketch section across a 'typical' continent, labelling all important features such as mountain belt, shield, shelf, etc. Compare your drawing with Figure 4.18.
3   List the main stages in an orogenic episode.
4   In the Caledonian orogenic belt in Britain, island arc volcanic rocks of Ordovician age are found at Ballantrae (just south of the Southern Uplands Fault, Fig. 5.3), in the Lake District and in North Wales. Also, blueschists and ocean floor rocks occur in Anglesey and at Ballantrae. What indication do these rock types give of plate activity during the Caledonian orogenic episode?
5   Using Table 5.1, explain the great differences in the amounts of sedimentary and metamorphic rocks in Precambrian and Phanerozoic mountain belts.

6 Suggest some reasons why greenstone belts are so named.

7 Why was heat production so much greater in the Archaean than today?

8 Find out some facts about the Moon, e.g. (a) what is its age?, (b) what is the composition at the surface? and (c) when was it most affected by meteorite impact cratering? From what you have learned in this chapter, mention some similarities between the early histories of the Earth and the Moon.

9 Why do only metamorphic rocks occur in areas where rocks of Archaean age are exposed?

6 The timing of metamorphic events

The aim of this final chapter is to draw together some of the ideas presented earlier and to emphasise the interrelations between deformation, metamorphic mineral growth and heat flow during mountain building.

Deformation and metamorphism often occur together, but not necessarily at exactly the same time. Fold movements may take place before, during or after a metamorphic event. The study of metamorphic rocks is complicated by the fact that rocks may be folded and metamorphosed several times, at different grades, during one orogenic episode. In fact this is the rule rather than the exception. Metamorphic mineral growth too can take place before, during or after deformation, depending on how temperature conditions varied during deformation. Deciphering a complex metamorphic and tectonic history is usually possible only when rocks are closely examined under the microscope. In the field it may be possible to observe porphyroblasts in metamorphic rocks. Relationships between porphyroblasts and the other minerals in a rock may provide some indications of the progress of metamorphism. For example, porphyroblasts may cut across a foliation defined by platy minerals. In this case, the porphyroblasts must have grown after deformation, in what is described as static growth, due to a temperature rise. The platy minerals, on the other hand, grew during deformation, as a result of which the rock has a directional fabric. This fabric is broken by the porphyroblasts, which grew in a random fashion (Fig. 6.1). Two episodes of oriented metamorphic mineral growth may occur if rocks are folded and metamorphosed more than once. Figure 6.2 shows an example of a folded gneiss in which an early gneissose banding formed by parallel oriented minerals has been later folded. During this later event, micas have grown parallel to the axial plane of the fold to give a directional fabric, known as an axial plane cleavage. In the hinge zone of the fold, this cleavage cuts across the earlier-formed fabric. It is possible to work out a complex history of mineral growth by examining mineral relations in this way, but since many of the relations can only be observed with the help of a petrological microscope, it is not appropriate to develop this further here. Before leaving the topic, though, it is useful at this point to refer back to Figure 4.15, which is a photograph of a rock

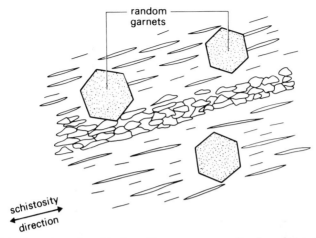

Figure 6.1   Garnet porphyroblasts cutting across an earlier formed fabric.

thin-section. The rock in question is a pyroxene–feldspar granulite, which has been affected by a later retrogressive metamorphic event which involved the addition of water. During this later event, a reaction between pyroxene and water led to the formation of amphibole, which crystallised as tiny grains along pyroxene grain boundaries, forming a rim or corona. If this process had continued to completion, the rock would have recrystallised completely and the pyroxene would have been totally replaced by amphibole.

By carrying out such detective work, it is possible to construct a time picture of metamorphic mineral growth during an orogeny. Figure 6.3 shows an example of this for growth of the index minerals of Barrow's and Buchan zones in the Dalradian rocks of Scotland. The shaded portions indicate the length of time that minerals grew, relative to deformational episodes. The broad part of each blob signifies the period of maximum growth of the particular mineral. It is evident from Figure 6.3 that most minerals grew between the second and third deformational episodes in a period of static growth (implying that there was a rise in temperature in that period). Note, though, that some minerals, such as biotite and garnet, started to grow towards the end of the first deformational event, continued growing during the second event when their growth was at a maximum, and had ceased crystallising by the start of the third event. During the third and fourth events, earlier-formed crystals would be deformed or replaced by new minerals.

The metamorphic history of a rock could be plotted on the familiar

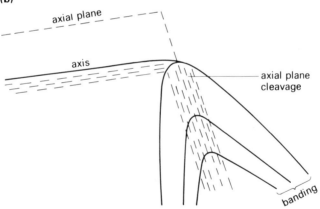

Figure 6.2   Axial plane cleavage in folded banded gneiss.

pressure–temperature graph. A study of mineral assemblages is used to provide pressure and temperature estimates at different times in the evolution of a metamorphic rock. The various pressure and temperature values are then connected by arrows to illustrate the changing conditions with time (Fig. 6.4). A graph like this is termed a pressure–temperature–time path. The path traces the history of a rock from burial through heating up and metamorphism to thrusting, uplift and exposure at the surface by erosion. The direction of the arrows on Figure 6.4

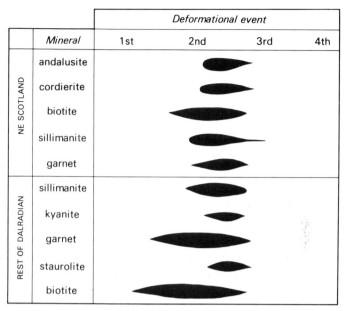

| | Mineral | Deformational event | | | |
		1st	2nd	3rd	4th
NE SCOTLAND	andalusite				
	cordierite				
	biotite				
	sillimanite				
	garnet				
REST OF DALRADIAN	sillimanite				
	kyanite				
	garnet				
	staurolite				
	biotite				

Figure 6.3 Periods of growth of main metamorphic minerals in relation to deformational episodes affecting Dalradian rocks in Scotland during the Caledonian orogeny.

indicates that pressure and temperature were decreasing with time. This is to be expected if the rock was being elevated to the surface over a period of millions of years. During an orogenic cycle, though, pressure and temperature do not both increase then decrease together, steadily. Instead, the picture is rather more complicated due to the time-lag involved in heating up rocks that have been buried. The sequence of events in an orogenic belt might be something like this:

(1) Cold rocks, deposited at the surface, are buried relatively quickly to some depth and are raised to some corresponding pressure at the same time.
(2) They are gradually heated up by heat from radioactive decay of their minerals and by conductive heat from the mantle.
(3) The crust is thickened, its surface becomes elevated and is immediately subject to erosion.
(4) As erosion progresses, the rocks are gradually elevated, and depth and pressure decrease steadily.
(5) Heat cannot be conducted away as fast as the rocks are rising, so

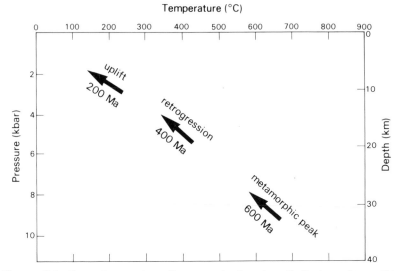

Figure 6.4 Press–temperature–time graph for hypothetical rocks metamorphosed 600 Ma ago.

they continue to be heated up and they reach some maximum temperature.

(6) Eventually heat loss starts to match the rate of uplift and erosion until the rocks have cooled down to surface temperatures as they are exposed there.

Because burial, heating and uplift do not take place at a constant rate, the geotherm during orogeny is not constant, but instead curves, the maximum curvature corresponding to (5) above, where the rocks reach their maximum temperature. In this example, the maximum temperature is not achieved when the rocks are at their greatest depth of burial.

Metasomatism – bulk chemical change

Throughout the discussion so far, it has been assumed that metamorphism has involved no overall change in the chemistry of rocks, other than the addition or subtraction of water and carbon dioxide. However, certain kinds of metamorphism do involve major changes in bulk chemistry, usually through the addition of components. **Metasomatism** is the term used to describe metamorphic processes in which substantial amounts of 'foreign' components are added to a host rock, usually with the aid of fluids (water, carbon dioxide, chlorine, fluorine, etc.) that act as carriers, transporting atoms and ions relatively large distances in a rock mass. The word is derived from Greek roots meaning 'change in body composition'. Metasomatism involves the diffusion of relatively mobile atoms and ions, such as potassium. Silica is another material which can be transported by hydrous fluids. Rock products of metasomatism may have unusual chemical compositions, due to the mixing of several components. Skarn deposits in certain contact aureoles, particularly those originating when granite has intruded limestone (e.g. the aureole of the Beinn an Dubhaich granite, p. 53), are thought to have resulted from metasomatic effects. In the example quoted from Skye, the fluid phase would have been carbon dioxide, which acted as the 'carrier'. Skarns may contain magnetite and sulphides of iron, zinc, lead and copper, in association with calcium-rich pyroxene and calcium-iron garnet. Limestones make particularly favourable hosts for skarns because calcium carbonate reacts readily with granite magma, causing a reduction in volume of the host rock. Some limestone is replaced by ore minerals, and fluids are able to penetrate the mass of the rock relatively easily.

Glossary

aluminosilicates The Al_2SiO_5 **polymorphs**, andalusite, kyanite and sillimanite.

amphibolite Hornblende-feldspar **gneiss**, often with garnet; hornblende or another amphibole predominates; result of high-grade regional metamorphism of basic lavas, tuffs, sills and dykes and also of impure, sandy, dolomitic limestone.

assemblage A group of minerals in equilibrium during metamorphism; the mineral content of a metamorphic rock.

asthenosphere Plastic layer in the upper mantle immediately beneath the **lithosphere** which allows movement of lithospheric **plates**.

augen gneiss Gneiss with large eye-shaped **porphyroblasts** of feldspar (usually) in a finer matrix of biotite, quartz and feldspar; **foliated** but not **banded**.

aureole *see* **contact aureole**.

banding Alternation of layers of different composition in metamorphic rocks, especially **gneisses**.

blueschist Metamorphic rock containing blue amphibole; usually basic igneous composition.

blueschist metamorphism High-pressure, low-temperature and low-heat flow metamorphism resulting in the formation of **blueschists**, often or usually above **subduction zones**.

breccia Fault rock consisting of angular crushed fragments of rock in fault zones.

brittle Type of deformation in which material snaps when stressed beyond its strength.

chiastolite Variety of andalusite in contact aureoles, showing cross-shaped arrangement of impurities.

cleavage Tendency to split or fracture into thin parallel sheets or plates.

component Chemical composition of a **phase** in a **system**.

contact aureole Heat affected zone of rocks around an igneous intrusion.

contact metamorphic rocks Rocks adjacent to and metamorphosed by the heat from an igneous intrusion.

country rocks Rocks surrounding an igneous intrusion.

craton Major mass of stable continental crust; usually equated with **shield**.

creep Permanent deformation with time resulting from the application of a constant **stress**.

crystal defect Discontinuity in the pattern of atoms or ions in a crystal lattice.

diagenesis Surface process involving compaction and cementation of sedimentary grains to give a sedimentary rock.

diffusion Free movement of material as atoms or ions through a solid rock during deformation and metamorphism.

directional fabric Metamorphic rock texture in which certain crystals display preferred orientation, due to **recrystallisation** during deformation.

ductile behaviour Deformation in which **strain** is distributed uniformly throughout the material being deformed. Ductile materials undergo permanent changes of shape without fracturing.

dynamic metamorphic rocks Rocks found in fault and thrust zones, formed by the action of high pressure, high strain and high fluid pressure.

elastic Property of a material to resume its original shape and size when the forces acting on it are removed, i.e. **strain** disappears when **stress** is removed.

fluid Liquid or gas.

foliation A **texture** of metamorphic rocks in which minerals are oriented in a planar fashion.

free energy Amount of energy that would be released or used up during a reversible process. The change in free energy is a controlling factor in metamorphic **reactions**.

geothermal gradient Rate of increase of temperature with depth in the Earth. Varies according to tectonic environment.

gneiss Coarse- to very coarse-grained **banded** rock with irregular **foliation** surfaces; does not split easily; minerals are segregated into light-coloured bands of quartz and feldspar and dark-coloured bands of biotite and hornblende, and possibly garnet.

gneissose banding Type of banding in metamorphic rocks in which quartz and feldspar bands alternate with bands of ferromagnesian minerals.

gradient Inclination of a slope, tangent to a curve.

granite gneiss Gneiss consisting almost entirely of quartz and feldspar, with a little biotite or hornblende; **foliated** but not strongly **banded**; originates from high-grade regional metamorphism of granitic rocks; occurs in fold mountain chains and abundantly in Precambrian **shields**.

granoblastic texture Metamorphic texture of equidimensional minerals and even grain size.

granulite Coarse, even-grained **granoblastic** rock, possibly **banded** on a large (0.5–1 m) scale, but not **foliated**; consists of pyroxene, plagioclase, quartz and garnet; sometimes referred to as pyroxene gneiss; derived from **high-pressure**, high-temperature regional metamorphism of sediments and igneous rocks involving extreme dehydration; found as small blocks in Precambrian **shields** and very rarely in young fold mountain chains.

greenstone belts Areas of Precambrian **shields** containing metamorphosed sediments and volcanic rocks, representing old sedimentary basins, intruded and bordered by granitic rocks.

half life Time taken for half the unstable isotopes of an element to decay.

heat flow Rate at which heat is lost from the interior of the Earth to the surface. Varies according to position on the crust.

hornblende schist Coarse-grained regionally metamorphosed dolerite or basalt made of hornblende and plagioclase showing pronounced lineation of hornblende needles, but schistosity is sometimes not well expressed.

hornfels Contact altered rock in thermal aureoles around large igneous intrusions; pelitic sediments and igneous rocks may be hornfelsed; fine-grained, hard, splintery rock. Low-grade hornfelses contain biotite, medium-grade, hornblende, high-grade, pyroxene.

index mineral Mineral in a sequence of metamorphic rocks indicating a **metamorphic zone**.

isograd Line on a map joining points of equal **metamorphic grade**; grade is defined in terms of index minerals.

lineation Arrangement of elements (e.g. minerals) in parallel lines; in metamorphic rocks, a **directional fabric**.

lithosphere Rigid outer part of the Earth, comprising the crust and part of the upper mantle, overlying the plastic **asthenosphere**.

marble Metamorphic rock derived from regional and contact metamorphism of calcite and dolomite limestones and impure carbonate sediments; coarse, even-grained **texture**; calcite marble is pure white; green and white streaky marble contains pyroxene, olivine and epidote; not **banded** or **foliated**; contact altered marbles may contain **skarn** deposits if intruded by granite.

metamorphic fabric A metamorphic **texture**, same as **directional fabric**.

metamorphic facies Subfields of the pressure–temperature field of metamorphism, based on characteristic mineral **assemblages**.

metamorphic grade Relative measure of intensity or level of metamorphism.

metamorphic zone Part of a sequence of metamorphic rocks characterised by a particular **index mineral** or **texture**.

metasomatism Type of metamorphism involving changes in bulk chemistry by the addition or removal of material.

migmatite Irregularly **banded**, streaky **gneiss** without strong **foliation**; consists of granitic (quartz and feldspar) veins, streaks and lenses among high-grade metamorphic rock, especially basic (hornblende and biotite) material; product of extreme high-grade regional metamorphism of sediments and igneous rocks, possibly resulting from **partial melting**; very common in Precambrian **shields**, associated with **gneiss**, granite and pegmatite.

mylonite Fine-grained, flinty, banded rock resulting from intense crushing, milling and recrystallising of rock in thrust zones; may show small-scale folds; may be rich in quartz.

orogenic belt Relatively long, narrow zone of crust containing folded and metamorphosed sediments and volcanic rocks, usually intruded by granitic plutons. The rocks of an orogenic belt have been uplifted and overthrust so that the belt shows positive relief.

orogenic cycle Time interval involving the formation, uplift and stabilisation of an **orogenic belt**.

overthrust Low angle reverse fault.

paired metamorphic belts Arrangement of metamorphic rocks in certain **orogenic belts** especially in the circum-Pacific region in which a high-pressure and a low pressure metamorphic belt occur side by side, the high-pressure belt being situated on the oceanic side of the associated low pressure belt. Presumed to be the result of underthrusting or subduction of an oceanic plate beneath an island arc or a continental margin.

partial melting Process in high pressure, high-temperature, high-water-pressure metamorphism whereby material with the lowest melting temperature melts first and separates out from the bulk of the rock; the lowest melting fraction is usually granitic in composition and granitic veins, sheets, patches and lenses may often characterise metamorphic rocks that have been involved in partial melting during their formation.

pelitic rock Shaly sedimentary rock and its metamorphosed equivalent.

phase Separate, distinct part of a **system**.

phyllite Medium-grained regionally metamorphosed **pelitic rock**, rich in green chlorite and mica; strongly **foliated**, splits less easily than **slate**, due to its being more sandy; foliation often crumpled by microfolds whose axes define a **lineation**.

plastic Property of a material to deform by flow once some critical stress value is reached.

plates Rigid, major segments of continental and oceanic **lithosphere** that are capable of slow movement over the plastic **asthenosphere** around the Earth's surface.

plate tectonics Theory that the Earth's **lithosphere** consists of a number of thin, rigid **plates** which move relative to one another, the movement being accommodated in the **asthenosphere**.

polymorphs Different crystalline forms of the same substance, e.g. the **aluminosilicates** (Al_2SiO_5) andalusite, kyanite and sillimanite.

pore fluid pressure Pressure exerted by fluids in pore spaces and along grain boundaries, expressed as a fraction of the total pressure.

porphyroblast Larger crystal of a mineral in a metamorphic rock in a finer grained groundmass.

porphyroblastic texture Metamorphic **texture** in which large crystals are set in a finer grained groundmass.

porphyroclast Large fragment of rock or mineral in a finer grained groundmass within a mylonite.

principal stresses A convenient way of expressing stress within the Earth as acting in three mutually perpendicular directions; referred to as maximum, intermediate and minimum principal stresses, one of which is usually vertical.

quartzite Recrystallised sandstone; regional and contact metamorphic rock; even-grained, **granoblastic**, glassy lustre, white or pinkish colour, hard and compact; high-grade quartzite may be **banded** (banded quartzite).

reaction Chemical activity between several **components**, yielding products.

recrystallisation Process whereby a mass of crystals is replaced by a new crystal aggregate of the same composition without melting or dissolution having taken place. Often used in the context of metamorphic processes as synonymous with crystallisation, in which new mineral **phases** grow as products of metamorphic **reactions**.

regional metamorphic rocks Metamorphic rocks occupying significantly large areas of the crust, formed under a variety of pressure and temperature conditions.

retrograde metamorphism Type of metamorphism involving replacement of a high-grade mineral **assemblage** by a lower grade assemblage at a later time; often with the addition of water.

schist Medium- to coarse-grained regionally metamorphosed **pelitic** sediment; contains abundant muscovite and, or biotite and quartz, frequently with red garnet; may show mineral **banding**; mica schist and garnet–mica schist are common names; schists possess a pronounced foliation called **schistosity**.

schistosity Type of directional fabric in which sheet silicates are arranged in a planar fashion.

serpentinite Regionally metamorphosed basic or ultrabasic igneous rock, later hydrated during retrogressive metamorphism; rather soft, dark-green, irregularly streaked and veined rock containing serpentine, talc, chlorite, calcite and iron ores.

shield Major structural feature of the Earth's crust, consisting of a large area and volume of metamorphic and igneous Precambrian rocks, which is stable and rigid and has remained practically unaffected by later orogenies.

skarn Rock formed by **metasomatism** at igneous contacts; may contain metal ores.

slate Fine-grained regionally metamorphosed **pelitic** sediment, rich in platy minerals; splits easily along **slaty cleavage** planes; bedding may be visible on cleavage planes; low grade of metamorphism.

slaty cleavage Ability of rock (**slate**) to be split into thin, planar sheets, due to planar arrangement of sheet silicates in **directional fabric**.

spotted rock Low-grade contact altered **pelitic** sediment or **slate**; spots consist of tiny clusters and patches of carbon, iron ore, biotite or **chiastolite**.

strain Deformation – ratio of change of shape, size or volume – resulting from the imposition of **stress**.

strain rate Amount of **strain** per unit time, usually expressed as x % per second.

stress Force per unit area; when a stress is applied to a body, a corresponding **strain** is produced.

subduction zone Long narrow belt on the crust in which oceanic crust is consumed or subducted by being forced into the mantle.

suture zone Narrow belt of deformed rocks marking an old continent–continent collision zone.

system A portion of material consisting of a number of **phases** and theoretically isolated for the study of possible changes in it under varied conditions.

tectonic cycle Cycle relating major crustal features to crustal movements and to the rocks formed as these features developed.

texture Relationship of size, shape and arrangement between minerals in a rock.

thermal metamorphism Recrystallisation of rocks due to addition of heat without **strain**; same as contact metamorphism.

xenolith Block of country rock incorporated in an igneous intrusion.

zeolites Group of pale coloured hydrated aluminium silicates of sodium, calcium and potassium. Form during burial, diagenesis and low-grade metamorphism (particularly of greywackes and basalts).

Further reading

Advanced Texts

Brown, G. C. and A. E. Mussett 1981. *The inaccessible Earth*. London: George Allen & Unwin.

Condie, K. C. 1976. *Plate tectonics and crustal evolution*. New York: Pergamon Press.

Gass, I. G., P. J. Smith and R. C. L. Wilson 1971. *Understanding the Earth*. Horsham, Sussex: Artemis Press.

Harris, A. L., C. H. Holland and B. E. Leake 1979. *The Caledonides of the British Isles – Reviewed*. Geol. Soc. London spec. publ., no. 8. London: The Geological Society.

Mason, R. 1978. *Petrology of the metamorphic rocks*. London: George Allen & Unwin.

Miyashiro, A. 1973. *Metamorphism and metamorphic belts*. London: George Allen & Unwin.

Spry, A. 1969. *Metamorphic textures*. Oxford: Pergamon Press.

The Open University 1972. *Science: a second level course. Geology. Block 4. Internal processes*. Milton Keynes: Open University Press.

The Open University 1980. *Science: a third level course. Case studies in Earth sciences. Crustal and mantle processes. Dalradian case study. Orogenic processes*. Milton Keynes: Open University Press.

Vernon, R. H. 1976. *Metamorphic processes: reactions and microstructure development*. London: George Allen & Unwin.

Weyman, D. 1981. *Tectonic processes*. London: George Allen & Unwin.

Windley, B. F. 1977. *The evolving continents*. Chichester: Wiley.

Wyllie, P. J. 1971. *The dynamic Earth*. New York: Wiley.

Wyllie, P. J. 1976. *The way the Earth works*. New York: Wiley.

Field guides to areas of metamorphic rocks in the British Isles

Anderson, T. B. 1978. *A traverse in the North-west Irish Caledonides*. Guide series, no. 3. Dublin: Geological Survey of Ireland.

Barber, A. J. 1978. *The Lewisian and Torridonian of North-west Scotland*. Geologists' Assn guide, no. 21. London: The Geologists' Association.

Bluck, B. J. 1973. *Excursion guide to the geology of the Glasgow district*. Glasgow: Geological Society of Glasgow.

Bruck, P. M. 1978. *The Caledonian and pre-Caledonian rocks of South-east Ireland*. Guide series, no. 2. Dublin: Geological Survey of Ireland.

Gill, G. 1978. *The Moray Firth area geological studies*. Inverness: Inverness Field Club.

Gribble, C. D. 1976. *Ardnamurchan, a guide to geological excursions*. Edinburgh: Geological Society of Edinburgh.

Institute of Geological Sciences 1978. *Description of 1 : 25 000 geological map sheet SO49, Church Stretton*. London: Institute of Geological Sciences.

Johnson, M. R. W. and I. Parsons 1979. *Macgregor and Phemister's geological excursion guide to the Assynt district of Sutherland*. Edinburgh: Geological Society of Edinburgh.

Lambert, R. S. J. 1964. *Guide to the Moine Schists and Lewisian Gneiss around Mallaig, Inverness-shire*. Geologists' Assn guide, no. 35. London: The Geologists' Association.

Macgregor, M. 1972. *Excursion guide to the geology of Arran*. Glasgow: Geological Society of Glasgow.

Read, H. H. 1960. *North-east Scotland: the Dalradian*. Geologists' Assn guide, no. 31. London: The Geologists' Association.

Roberts, B. 1979. *The geology of Snowdonia and Llŷn: an outline and field guide*. Bristol: Hilger.

Roberts, J. L. and J. E. Treagus 1977. The Dalradian rocks of the South-west Highlands – introduction. Collection of 7 excursion guides. *Scott. J. Geol.* **13**, 85–184.

Answers to exercises

Chapter 2

2.1 Platy minerals grow perpendicular to maximum stress direction; prismatic minerals grow parallel to stretching direction and, or fold axes. Deformation during metamorphism is implied.

2.2 From volcanic activity at the surface and from laboratory experiments on rocks and minerals involving stability at varying pressures and temperatures.

2.3 X-ray tracer (e.g. iodine), cancer therapy (radium treatment) in medicine; uranium for nuclear reactors and weapons; radiometric dating of rocks.

2.4 Pitch, treacle, glycerine, water: most viscous to least.

2.5 The ball bearing would fall faster in each case, i.e. the viscosity is reduced by a rise in temperature.

2.7 There is a similarity because mid-ocean ridges are younger than trenches by 100–150 Ma.

Chapter 3

3.1 A, spotted shale; B, hornfels with biotite; C, marble with dolomite and calcite. X, inside or outside the aureole (limestone or marble); Y, outer aureole (shale); Z, inner aureole (shale).

3.3 Chlorite (low), biotite, garnet (medium), kyanite, sillimanite (high).

Chapter 4

4.1 Schistosity would develop, and banding; a lineation might appear; hornblende and feldspar would grow (also some garnet and biotite). The rock might be called a hornblende–feldspar gneiss. Retrogressive metamorphism.

4.3 (a)–(5), (b)–(3) or (1), (c)–(6), (d)–(2), (e)–(7).

4.4 (a) marble or calc-schist; (b) pyroxene gneiss; (c) schist.

4.5 (a) calcite + amphibole + diopside + epidote (+ plagioclase); (b) pyroxene + plagioclase; (c) mica + quartz + garnet + andalusite (+ plagioclase).

Chapter 5

5.1 Metamorphic rocks are not found in mid-oceanic ridges. They are submarine mountain chains.

5.3 Deposition and burial of thick clastic sediments in a major sedimentary basin or geosyncline; folding, compression and closing of basin; crustal shortening and thickening; metamorphism, plutonic and volcanic igneous activity; uplift, stabilisation and erosion.

5.4 The rocks indicate that an ocean was subducted beneath the Northern and Southern zones of the Caledonian mountain belt as two continents collided.

5.5 Precambrian crust shows a deep section through the Earth; some metasediments are found, but the level of erosion is 20–40 km deep, so that overlying sediments would have been eroded away.

5.6 Greenstone belts contain abundant greenschists, amphibolites and hornblende schists.

5.7 Because of the greater abundance of radioactive isotopes.

5.8 (a) 4500 Ma; (b) basalt and anorthosite; (c) 4000–3800 Ma ago. The Earth–Moon system probably went through the same history in the period 4500–4000 Ma ago, but the internal structure of the Earth (mainly the presence of the mobile upper mantle) meant that the histories of the Earth and Moon had diverged by at least 4000 Ma ago.

5.9 Because the level of erosion is 30–40 km. Pressures and temperatures at such depths would have been 8–11 kb and 600–800 °C in the Archaean; no rock could escape metamorphism under such conditions.

Index

Entries in *italics* refer to figure numbers.